What does the Bible say about?

By Douglas Russell

Contents

What does the Bible say about?

Dedicated to:

Almighty God: Father, Son and Holy Spirit. Thine be the power, glory and honour. Forever and ever.

Amen

Acknowledgements:

I wish to acknowledge the following Christian brothers and sisters for their tireless work for God's kingdom and for their clear teaching that has enabled me write to this book:

Dr. Kent Hovind of Creation Science Evangelism, Lenox, Alabama, USA

Dr. Ken Ham of Answers in Genesis, Petersburg, Kentucky, USA

Dr. John MacArthur of Grace Community Church, Sun Valley, California, USA

The late David Pawson – Theologian

Fight For Truth – YouTube channel

In2 the LIGHT – YouTube channel

Spencer Smith – Pastor and YouTube channel

Mike Winger – Pastor and YouTube channel

www.biblehub.com – Online Bible resource

www.gotquestions.org – Christian apologetics website.

And the following for their encouragement and support:

Oliver F., brother and brother in Christ who edited this book

Mel F., sister in Christ and sister in law

Laura R., sister in Christ

Peter S, brother in Christ.

Preface

The primary purpose of this book is to exhort Christians to read their bibles. To be Berean Christians as commended by the apostle Paul is to examine the scriptures to determine the truth. I would do the same. Do not just believe what I say but compare it to scripture.

This is not intended as an exhaustive collection of all biblical texts on a particular topic but rather a selection of the clearest examples that can been found therein.

It is to assure you, the Christian reader, of the truth of God's Word and its inspiration, inerrancy and infallibility. It should also encourage all to just pick up the Bible and read it and know that they can trust it.

I do not directly intend it to offend or aggravate my brothers and sisters in the differing denominations in the UK regarding some of the topics I intend to discuss but I accept that it might happen.

Indeed, the main thrust of my writing is not to offend but rather present clearly what the Bible has to say regarding current issues affecting the church in the 21st century, to stand against liberalism and general ignorance of scripture, and to present answers scripturally rather than avoid discussions that may cause division.

We cannot rely on our feelings. As mature Christians we should find that as scripture teaches us, our opinions and beliefs should come more into line with what scripture clearly states. We ought to submit to scripture as the final authority and source of absolute truth until our glorious Saviour returns for his millennial reign.

I have been walking the narrow way for almost a decade and during my walk, I have met many fellow believers who believe in things that are clearly contrary to scripture or are otherwise generally ignorant of what it teaches. And whilst not primary doctrinal issues, there is clarity.

One result of leaders in the church avoiding contentious issues is that church members seeking biblical truth and clarity will go further afield and often outside the local church, away from the accepted orthodoxy to independent ministries, which teach them on these issues, to the detriment of the local church.

I am unapologetically a reader of the King James Bible when it comes to Biblical authority. I believe it is where God chose to preserve his Word (see Psalm 8) in the English language.

"Study to shew thyself approved unto God, a workman that needeth not to be ashamed, rightly dividing the word of truth" 2 Tim 2:15.

"All scripture is given by inspiration of God, and is profitable for doctrine, for reproof, for correction, for instruction in righteousness" 2 Tim 3:16.

"In the mouth of two or three witnesses shall every word be established" 2 Corinthians 13:1.

"No scripture has private interpretation" 2 Peter 1.

"For the invisible things of him from the creation of the world are clearly seen, being understood by the things that are made, even his eternal power and Godhead; so that they are without excuse:" Romans 1:20.

Introduction

Before reading each chapter, may I recommend you retreat somewhere quiet, where you can be alone with the Lord and pray, and ask the Holy Spirit to guide you to the truth regarding the topic of each chapter. For the Lord in his grace has granted me much clarity on the topics covered in this booklet.

Nowadays Christians seem to pitch Bible verses against one another, selecting the ones they like and disregarding the ones they don't (or the ones that disagree with their preferred one).

This is bad exegesis. No verse has a private (personal) interpretation. One cannot cherry-pick verses from scripture. All verses on a particular topic need to be considered as a whole.

Verses on a particular subject must be blended together in a way that they don't contradict each other in order to get a full understanding of the meaning. One ought to compare scripture with scripture.

For example, one cannot use Galatians 3:28: "There is neither Jew nor Greek, there is neither bond nor free, there is neither male nor female: for ye are all one in Christ Jesus."

as a proof text that women can be elders in the church as that would contradict 1 Timothy 3:1:

"This is a true saying, If a man desire the office of a bishop, he desireth a good work."

Each chapter will focus on one topic and will present selected, relevant passages from the Bible, in full from the King James Version, so you can read for yourself what scripture says before I comment. All I ask is you put aside your own views and just allow scripture to talk to you.

All passages from the King James Version are printed verbatim so include 17th century grammar and punctuation.

Abortion

GENESIS 1:26-28

And God said, Let us make man in our image, after our likeness: and let them have dominion over the fish of the sea, and over the fowl of the air, and over the cattle, and over all the earth, and over every creeping thing that creepeth upon the earth. So God created man in his own image, in the image of God created he him; male and female created he them. And God blessed them, and God said unto them, Be fruitful, and multiply, and replenish the earth, and subdue it: and have dominion over the fish of the sea, and over the fowl of the air, and over every living thing that moveth upon the earth

GENESIS 5:1-2

This is the book of the generations of Adam. In the day that God created man, in the likeness of God made he him; Male and female created he them; and blessed them, and called their name Adam, in the day when they were created.

GENESIS 9:1-7

And God blessed Noah and his sons, and said unto them, Be fruitful, and multiply, and replenish the earth. And the fear of you and the dread of you shall be upon every beast of the earth, and upon every fowl of the air, upon all that moveth upon the earth, and upon all the fishes of the sea; into your hand are they delivered. Every moving thing that liveth shall be meat for you; even as the green herb have I given you all things. But flesh with the life thereof, which is the blood thereof, shall ye not eat. And surely your blood of your lives will I require; at the hand of every beast will I require it, and at the hand of man; at the hand of every man's brother will I require the life of man. Whoso sheddeth man's blood, by man shall his blood be shed: for in the image of God made he man. And you, be ye fruitful, and multiply; bring forth abundantly in the earth, and multiply therein.

GENESIS 15:1-6

After these things the word of the LORD came unto Abram in a vision, saying, Fear not, Abram: I am thy shield, and thy exceeding great reward. And Abram said, Lord GOD, what wilt thou give me, seeing I go childless, and the steward of my house is this Eliezer of Damascus? And Abram said, Behold, to me thou hast given no seed: and, lo, one born in my house is mine heir. And, behold, the word of the LORD came unto him, saying, This shall not be thine heir; but he that shall come forth out of thine own bowels shall be thine heir. And he brought him forth abroad, and said, Look now toward heaven, and tell the stars, if thou be able to number them: and he said unto him, So shall thy seed be. And he believed in the LORD; and he counted it to him for righteousness.

GENESIS 25:21–23

Isaac pleaded with the LORD on behalf of his wife, because she was unable to have children. The LORD answered Isaac's prayer, and Rebekah became pregnant with twins. But the two children struggled with each other in her womb. So she went to ask the LORD about it. "Why is this happening to me?" she asked. And the LORD told her, "The sons in your womb will become two nations. From the very beginning, the two nations will be rivals. One nation will be stronger than the other; and your older son will serve your younger son."

EXODUS 20:13

Thou shalt not kill.

EXODUS 21:22–25

If men strive, and hurt a woman with child, so that her fruit depart from her, and yet no mischief follow: he shall be surely punished, according as the woman's husband will lay upon him; and he shall pay as the judges determine. And if any mischief follow, then thou shalt give life for life, Eye for eye, tooth for tooth, hand for hand, foot for foot, Burning for burning, wound for wound, stripe for stripe.

LEVITICUS 18:21

And thou shalt not let any of thy seed pass through the fire to Molech, neither shalt thou profane the name of thy God: I am the LORD.

LEVITICUS 20:1–5

And the LORD spake unto Moses, saying, Again, thou shalt say to the children of Israel, Whosoever he be of the children of Israel, or of the strangers that sojourn in Israel, that giveth any of his seed unto Molech; he shall surely be put to death: the people of the land shall stone him with stones. And I will set my face against that man, and will cut him off from among his people; because he hath given of his seed unto Molech, to defile my sanctuary, and to profane my holy name. And if the people of the land do any ways hide their eyes from the man, when he giveth of his seed unto Molech, and kill him not: Then I will set my face against that man, and against his family, and will cut him off, and all that go a whoring after him, to commit whoredom with Molech, from among their people.

DEUTERONOMY 5:17

Thou shalt not kill.

DEUTERONOMY 7:12-14

Wherefore it shall come to pass, if ye hearken to these judgments, and keep, and do them, that the LORD thy God shall keep unto thee the covenant and the mercy which he sware unto thy fathers: And he will love thee, and bless thee, and multiply thee: he will also bless the fruit of thy womb, and the fruit of thy land, thy corn, and thy wine, and thine oil, the increase of thy kine, and the flocks of thy sheep, in the land which he sware unto thy fathers to give thee. Thou shalt be blessed above all people: there shall not be male or female barren among you, or among your cattle.

JUDGES 16:16–17

And it came to pass, when she pressed him daily with her words, and urged him, so that his soul was vexed unto death; That he told her all his heart, and said unto her, There hath not come a rasor upon mine head; for I have been a Nazarite unto God from my mother's womb: if I be shaven, then my strength will go from me, and I shall become weak, and be like any other man.

RUTH 4:13–15

So Boaz took Ruth, and she was his wife: and when he went in unto her, the LORD gave her conception, and she bare a son. And the women said unto Naomi, Blessed be the LORD, which hath not left thee this day without a kinsman, that his name may be famous in Israel. And he shall be unto thee a restorer of thy life, and a nourisher of thine old age: for thy daughter in law, which loveth thee, which is better to thee than seven sons, hath born him.

2 SAMUEL 12:21–23

Then said his servants unto him, What thing is this that thou hast done? thou didst fast and weep for the child, while it was alive; but when the child was dead, thou didst rise and eat bread. And he said, While the child was yet alive, I fasted and wept: for I said, Who can tell whether GOD will be gracious to me, that the child may live? But now he is dead, wherefore should I fast? can I bring him back again? I shall go to him, but he shall not return to me.

JOB 10:8–12

Thine hands have made me and fashioned me together round about; yet thou dost destroy me. Remember, I beseech thee, that thou hast made me as the clay; and wilt thou bring me into dust again? Hast thou not poured me out as milk, and curdled me like cheese? Thou hast clothed me with skin and flesh, and hast fenced me with bones and sinews. Thou hast granted me life and favour, and thy visitation hath preserved my spirit.

JOB 31:15

Did not he that made me in the womb make him? and did not one fashion us in the womb?

JOB 33:4

The Spirit of God hath made me, and the breath of the Almighty hath given me life.

PSALM 18-30-32

As for God, his way is perfect: the word of the LORD is tried: he is a buckler to all those that trust in him. For who is God save the LORD? or who is a rock save our God? It is God that girdeth me with strength, and maketh my way perfect.

PSALM 51:5

Behold, I was shapen in iniquity; and in sin did my mother conceive me.

PSALM 104:30

Thou sendest forth thy spirit, they are created: and thou renewest the face of the earth.

PSALM 119:73

Thy hands have made me and fashioned me: give me understanding, that I may learn thy commandments.

PSALM 127:3-5

Lo, children are an heritage of the LORD: and the fruit of the womb is his reward. As arrows are in the hand of a mighty man; so are children of the youth. Happy is the man that hath his quiver full of them: they shall not be ashamed, but they shall speak with the enemies in the gate.

PSALM 139:12-16

Yea, the darkness hideth not from thee; but the night shineth as the day: the darkness and the light are both alike to thee. For thou hast possessed my reins: thou hast covered me in my mother's womb.I will praise thee; for I am fearfully and wonderfully made: marvellous are thy works; and that my soul knoweth right well. My substance was not hid from thee, when I was made in secret, and curiously wrought in the lowest parts of the earth. Thine eyes did see my substance, yet being unperfect; and in thy book all my members were written, which in continuance were fashioned, when as yet there was none of them.

ECCLESIASTES 5:15

As he came forth of his mother's womb, naked shall he return to go as he came, and shall take nothing of his labour, which he may carry away in his hand.

ISAIAH 45:1–5

Listen, O isles, unto me; and hearken, ye people, from far; The LORD hath called me from the womb; from the bowels of my mother hath he made mention of my name. And he hath made my mouth like a sharp sword; in the shadow of his hand hath he hid me, and made me a polished shaft; in his quiver hath he hid me; And said unto me, Thou art my servant, O Israel, in whom I will be glorified. Then I said, I have laboured in vain, I have spent my strength for nought, and in vain: yet surely my judgment is with the LORD, and my work with my God. And now, saith the LORD that formed me from the womb to be his servant, to bring Jacob again to him, Though Israel be not gathered, yet shall I be glorious in the eyes of the LORD, and my God shall be my strength.

JEREMIAH 1:4–5

Then the word of the LORD came unto me, saying, Before I formed thee in the belly I knew thee; and before thou camest forth out of the womb I sanctified thee, and I ordained thee a prophet unto the nations.

EZEKIEL 18:20

The soul that sinneth, it shall die. The son shall not bear the iniquity of the father, neither shall the father bear the iniquity of the son: the righteousness of the righteous shall be upon him, and the wickedness of the wicked shall be upon him.

MATTHEW 1:18–21

Now the birth of Jesus Christ was on this wise: When as his mother Mary was espoused to Joseph, before they came together, she was found with child of the Holy Ghost. Then Joseph her husband, being a just man, and not willing to make her a publick example, was minded to put her away privily. But while he thought on these things, behold, the angel of the Lord appeared unto him in a dream, saying, Joseph, thou son of David, fear not to take unto thee Mary thy wife: for that which is conceived in her is of the Holy Ghost. And she shall bring forth a son, and thou shalt call his name JESUS: for he shall save his people from their sins.

MATTHEW 22:34-40

But when the Pharisees had heard that he had put the Sadducees to silence, they were gathered together. Then one of them, which was a lawyer, asked him a question, tempting him, and saying, Master, which is the great commandment in the law? Jesus said unto him, Thou shalt love the Lord thy God with all thy heart, and with all thy soul, and with all thy mind. This is the first and great commandment. And the second is like unto it, Thou shalt love thy neighbour as thyself. On these two commandments hang all the law and the prophets.

LUKE 1:39-45

And Mary arose in those days, and went into the hill country with haste, into a city of Juda; And entered into the house of Zacharias, and saluted Elisabeth. And it came to pass, that, when Elisabeth heard the salutation of Mary, the babe leaped in her womb; and Elisabeth was filled with the Holy Ghost: And she spake out with a loud voice, and said, Blessed art thou among women, and blessed is the fruit of thy womb. And whence is this to me, that the mother of my Lord should come to me? For, lo, as soon as the voice of thy salutation sounded in mine ears, the babe leaped in my womb for joy. And blessed is she that believed: for there shall be a performance of those things which were told her from the Lord.

ROMANS 6:1-7

What shall we say then? Shall we continue in sin, that grace may abound? God forbid. How shall we, that are dead to sin, live any longer therein? Know ye not, that so many of us as were baptized into Jesus Christ were baptized into his death? Therefore we are buried with him by baptism into death: that like as Christ was raised up from the dead by the glory of the Father, even so we also should walk in newness of life. For if we have been planted together in the likeness of his death, we shall be also in the likeness of his resurrection: Knowing this, that our old man is crucified with him, that the body of sin might be destroyed, that henceforth we should not serve sin. For he that is dead is freed from sin.

ROMANS 13:8-10

Owe no man any thing, but to love one another: for he that loveth another hath fulfilled the law. For this, Thou shalt not commit adultery, Thou shalt not kill, Thou shalt not steal, Thou shalt not bear false witness, Thou shalt not covet; and if there be any other commandment, it is briefly comprehended in this saying, namely, Thou shalt love thy neighbour as thyself. Love worketh no ill to his neighbour: therefore love is the fulfilling of the law.

GALATIANS 1:15–16

But when it pleased God, who separated me from my mother's womb, and called me by his grace, To reveal his Son in me, that I might preach him among the heathen; immediately I conferred not with flesh and blood:

1 JOHN 3:13–17

Marvel not, my brethren, if the world hate you. We know that we have passed from death unto life, because we love the brethren. He that loveth not his brother abideth in death. Whosoever hateth his brother is a murderer: and ye know that no murderer hath eternal life abiding in him. Hereby perceive we the love of God, because he laid down his life for us: and we ought to lay down our lives for the brethren. But whoso hath this world's good, and seeth his brother have need, and shutteth up his bowels of compassion from him, how dwelleth the love of God in him?

This is probably the most emotive and sensitive topic in society today, with strong feelings on both sides and whilst the Bible does not explicitly mention the topic of abortion, there are plenty verses that tell us what God thinks about it. Let us consider the following questions:

What does the Bible say about unborn babies?

Is it wrong to kill?

Are there any exceptions i.e. for rape or incest?

We do not have to read far into the Bible before we are told about the nature of life in the womb. Genesis 25:21 gives the description of Isaac's wife, Rebekah being unable to have children. In faith, Isaac prays to God, who in turn hears the prayer and Rebekah becomes pregnant with sons. Even before they are born the Bible tells us that they struggled with each other in the womb, causing Rebekah to ask God why it was happening to her. God says that the

15

two sons will become two nations who will always be rivals. God knows what the two children will become, before they are even born.

The book of Psalms has much to say the nature of life in the womb, and what happens within it:

Psalm 119 tells us that God himself fashions us inside the womb, that we are the work of his hands. This may be a metaphor – that we develop in his image to his ordained plan or that he himself actually is involved in our development, even before conception. (Jeremiah 1:4).

Psalm 127 tells us that children are an inheritance from the Lord, the fruit of the womb being a reward. Children are likened to a quiver of arrows, and joyful is the man with many arrows.

Psalm 139 expounds on God's involvement in the development of the fetus, that God "possessed my reins", the 'reins' being the inwards parts – as a more modern reading would put it – which the Hebrews believed to be the first parts of the baby formed in the womb, and 'possessed' set straight or created.

It is God himself who knits us together in the womb, and he can see the work of his hands in the darkness of the womb. He also records all days of our yet unlived lives.

Isaiah 45 also touches upon God's foreknowledge of the life of the child in the womb, when Isaiah says that God called him from the womb, from the bowels of his mother he has mentioned his name.

Jeremiah 1 has a similar statement in that God tells Jeremiah that he knew Jeremiah before he formed him in his mother's womb and that before he was born, he was sanctified and ordained to be a prophet.

Babies are a blessing, reward and a gift from God, who is there at the moment of conception, forming them with his own hands. Indeed, Genesis 1, Genesis 5 and Genesis 9 tell us that God made us in his own image, male and female. We therefore are image bearers of God. We bare his likeness morally, spiritually and intellectually.

Furthermore in Luke 1, the baby in Elizabeth's womb leaps for joy when Elizabeth hears Mary's greeting, and in Psalm 51, David writes that he was conceived in sin. Babies in the womb then have joy and sin, so they are no different to the rest of us who have been born, they have the same level of humanity.

Genesis 9 and the Mosaic covenant gives us our first law related to the sin of murder: the murderer's life is forfeit. This command is repeated in Exodus 20 with a simple "Thou shalt not kill", one of the ten commandments, which are also known as the moral law. They apply to all mankind. The penalty for murder in the Old Testament is death. Eye for eye, tooth for tooth; the punishment matching the crime.

Exodus 21 then gives us a clear example of a situation where an injury to a pregnant women causes her to give birth prematurely.

"If men strive, and hurt a woman with child, so that her fruit depart from her, and yet no mischief follow: he shall be surely punished, according as the woman's husband will lay upon him; and he shall pay as the judges determine. And if any mischief follow, then thou shalt give life for life, Eye for eye, tooth for tooth, hand for hand, foot for foot, Burning for burning, wound for wound, stripe for stripe."

This is a very pertinent passage to this discussion as it clearly doesn't differentiate between the injury or death of the woman and that of her baby i.e. it treats them equally. It simply says that where the baby is premature due to violence to the woman, but both her and her baby survive – and yet no mischief follow – then the perpetrator of the act must pay a fine that the judges and the woman's husband decide. However if anything does happen to the women or the baby, then it's eye for eye, tooth for tooth, which would mean a life for a life. This also means the murder of a pregnant women amounts to a double murder.

The command not to kill is repeated again in Romans 13. Paul tells us that if we truly loved our neighbours as ourselves, then we would keep the commandments. This passage picks up on what Jesus says in Matthew 22 when he states that the greatest command is to love the Lord your

God with all your heart, soul and mind. And the second being to love your neighbour as yourself.

So what should happen in the case of rape or incest resulting in pregnancy? Well, following the Old Testament example the rapist would be executed. Ezekiel 18 tells us that the son should not bear the responsibility for the sin of the father, neither should the father bear responsibility for the sin of the son. So the baby conceived during rape or incest should not be punished (killed) for the crime committed by the father. No person innocent of any crime should be punished.

1 John tells us that we ought to lay down our lives for our brothers, just as Jesus laid down his life for sinners. And if we don't love one another then we are not truly believers. The unborn are just as much our brothers as born human beings, and we ought to protect them.

People will protest 'What about the victim's feelings?' 'Think about the trauma caused to the woman, having to give birth to the baby of her rapist!'

One's personal feelings do not determine what's right and wrong. Morality needs a standard outside ourselves. This is why God gave us the 10 commandments. He establishes objective morality. His ways are perfect (Psalm 18). It does not matter what human jurisprudence says. God's law takes precedence.

The choice to have the baby seems to determine whether one believes the baby has intrinsic value or not. If the pregnancy is wanted then it is a baby. If it is not wanted then it is just a clump of cells that can be discarded. In actual fact, in this context the only difference between a baby in the womb and you or I is age, location and level of development.

Abortion is the killing of the unborn based on a mother's unilateral judgement and choice. Such unprovoked killing of a defenceless, unborn baby is unethical and should be defined as murder in any society.

To conclude, abortion is not the unforgivable sin. Women who've had an abortion, men who've encouraged or pressured women to have one and doctors who've performed one, can all be forgiven. But this is totally different to saying it's OK to have an abortion because God will forgive me. This is an abuse of grace. Abortion is a sin.

The Apostle Paul says:

"What shall we say then? Shall we continue in sin, that grace may abound? God forbid. How shall we, that are dead to sin, live any longer therein?" ROMANS 6:1–2

Shall we go on sinning so more grace abounds? Certainly not!
There is freedom in Christ but not all choices we are free to make are good for us or have positive outcomes. The Old Testament can guide us in these decisions.

In short, abortion is a sin as it is the murder of an unborn human being.

Anglican Communion/Church of England (CoE)
Generally opposes abortion, with very few exceptions

Roman Catholicism/Orthodox

Teaches abortion is a sin but accepts certain medical procedures like chemotherapy or a hysterectomy can indirectly lead to the death of the unborn.

Baptists

Take a variety of views from strongly opposed to moderately opposed, with an exception only being for the life of the mother.

Methodists

Take a moderate anti-abortion position, and state whilst abortion should not be available on demand, it should remain subject to a legal framework, to responsible counselling and to medical judgement.

Baptism

MATTHEW 28:19

Go ye therefore, and teach all nations, baptizing them in the name of the Father, and of the Son, and of the Holy Ghost:

MARK 1:4-11

John did baptize in the wilderness, and preach the baptism of repentance for the remission of sins. And there went out unto him all the land of Judaea, and they of Jerusalem, and were all baptized of him in the river of Jordan, confessing their sins. And John was clothed with camel's hair and with a girdle of a skin about his loins; and he did eat locusts and wild honey; And preached, saying, There cometh one mightier than I after me, the latchet of whose shoes I am not worthy to stoop down and unloose. I indeed have baptized you with water: but he shall baptize you with the Holy Ghost. And it came to pass in those days, that Jesus came from Nazareth of Galilee, and was baptized of John in Jordan. And straightway coming up out of the water, he saw the heavens opened, and the Spirit like a dove descending upon him: And there came a voice from heaven, saying, Thou art my beloved Son, in whom I am well pleased.

LUKE 3:21–22

Now when all the people were baptized, it came to pass, that Jesus also being baptized, and praying, the heaven was opened, And the Holy Ghost descended in a bodily shape like a dove upon him, and a voice came from heaven, which said, Thou art my beloved Son; in thee I am well pleased.

ACTS 2:36-41

Therefore let all the house of Israel know assuredly, that God hath made that same Jesus, whom ye have crucified, both Lord and Christ. Now when they heard this, they were pricked in their heart, and said unto Peter and to the rest of the apostles, Men and brethren, what shall we do? Then Peter said unto them, Repent, and be baptized every one of you in the name of Jesus Christ for the remission of sins, and ye shall receive the gift of the Holy Ghost. For the promise is unto you, and to your children, and to all that are afar off, even as many as the Lord our God shall call.

And with many other words did he testify and exhort, saying, Save yourselves from this untoward generation. Then they that gladly received his word were baptized: and the same day there were added unto them about three thousand souls.

ACTS 8:26–39

And the angel of the Lord spake unto Philip, saying, Arise, and go toward the south unto the way that goeth down from Jerusalem unto Gaza, which is desert. And he arose and went: and, behold, a man of Ethiopia, an eunuch of great authority under Candace queen of the Ethiopians, who had the charge of all her treasure, and had come to Jerusalem for to worship, Was returning, and sitting in his chariot read Esaias the prophet. Then the Spirit said unto Philip, Go near, and join thyself to this chariot. And Philip ran thither to him, and heard him read the prophet Esaias, and said, Understandest thou what thou readest? And he said, How can I, except some man should guide me? And he desired Philip that he would come up and sit with him. The place of the scripture which he read was this, He was led as a sheep to the slaughter; and like a lamb dumb before his shearer, so opened he not his mouth: In his humiliation his judgment was taken away: and who shall declare his generation? for his life is taken from the earth. And the eunuch answered Philip, and said, I pray thee, of whom speaketh the prophet this? of himself, or of some other man? Then Philip opened his mouth, and began at the same scripture, and preached unto him Jesus. And as they went on their way, they came unto a certain water: and the eunuch said, See, here is water; what doth hinder me to be baptized? And Philip said, If thou believest with all thine heart, thou mayest. And he answered and said, I believe that Jesus Christ is the Son of God. And he commanded the chariot to stand still: and they went down both into the water, both Philip and the eunuch; and he baptized him. And when they were come up out of the water, the Spirit of the Lord caught away Philip, that the eunuch saw him no more: and he went on his way rejoicing.

ACTS 16:14

And a certain woman named Lydia, a seller of purple, of the city of Thyatira, which worshipped God, heard us: whose heart the Lord opened, that she attended unto the things which were spoken of Paul. And when she was baptized, and her household, she besought us, saying, If ye have judged me to be faithful to the Lord, come into my house, and abide there. And she constrained us.

ACTS 16:25-34

And at midnight Paul and Silas prayed, and sang praises unto God: and the prisoners heard them. And suddenly there was a great earthquake, so that the foundations of the prison were shaken: and immediately all the doors were opened, and every one's bands were loosed. And the keeper of the prison awaking out of his sleep, and seeing the prison doors open, he drew out his sword, and would have killed himself, supposing that the prisoners had been fled. But Paul cried with a loud voice, saying, Do thyself no harm: for we are all here. Then he called for a light, and sprang in, and came trembling, and fell down before Paul and Silas, And brought them out, and said, Sirs, what must I do to be saved? And they said, Believe on the Lord Jesus Christ, and thou shalt be saved, and thy house. And they spake unto him the word of the Lord, and to all that were in his house. And he took them the same hour of the night, and washed their stripes; and was baptized, he and all his, straightway. And when he had brought them into his house, he set meat before them, and rejoiced, believing in God with all his house.

ACTS 18:8

And Crispus, the chief ruler of the synagogue, believed on the Lord with all his house; and many of the Corinthians hearing believed, and were baptized.

ACTS 19:1-7

And it came to pass, that, while Apollos was at Corinth, Paul having passed through the upper coasts came to Ephesus: and finding certain disciples, He said unto them, Have ye received the Holy Ghost since ye believed? And they said unto him, We have not so much as heard whether there be any Holy Ghost. And he said unto them, Unto what then were ye baptized? And they said, Unto John's baptism. Then said Paul, John verily baptized with the baptism of repentance, saying unto the people, that they should believe on him which should come after him, that is, on Christ Jesus. When they heard this, they were baptized in the name of the Lord Jesus. And when Paul had laid his hands upon them, the Holy Ghost came on them;

and they spake with tongues, and prophesied. And all the men were about twelve.

EPHESIANS 4:4-6
There is one body, and one Spirit, even as ye are called in one hope of your calling; One Lord, one faith, one baptism, One God and Father of all, who is above all, and through all, and in you all.

ROMANS 6:1-10
What then shall we say? Shall we continue in sin so that grace may increase? Certainly not! How can we who died to sin live in it any longer? Or aren't you aware that all of us who were baptized into Christ Jesus were baptized into His death? We were therefore buried with Him through baptism into death, in order that, just as Christ was raised from the dead through the glory of the Father, we too may walk in newness of life. For if we have been united with Him like this in His death, we will certainly also be united with Him in His resurrection. We know that our old self was crucified with Him so that the body of sin might be rendered powerless, that we should no longer be slaves to sin. For anyone who has died has been freed from sin. Now

if we died with Christ, we believe that we will also live with Him. For we know that since Christ was raised from the dead, He cannot die again; death no longer has dominion over Him. The death He died, He died to sin once for all; but the life He lives, He lives to God

ROMANS 10:8-17

The word is nigh thee, even in thy mouth, and in thy heart: that is, the word of faith, which we preach; That if thou shalt confess with thy mouth the Lord Jesus, and shalt believe in thine heart that God hath raised him from the dead, thou shalt be saved. For with the heart man believeth unto righteousness; and with the mouth confession is made unto salvation. For the scripture saith, Whosoever believeth on him shall not be ashamed. For there is no difference between the Jew and the Greek: for the same Lord over all is rich unto all that call upon him. For whosoever shall call upon the name of the Lord shall be saved. How then shall they call on him in whom they have not believed? and how shall they believe in him of whom they have not heard? and how shall they hear without a preacher? And how shall they preach, except they be sent? as it is written, How beautiful are the feet of them that preach the gospel of peace, and bring glad tidings of good things! But they have not all obeyed the gospel. For Esaias saith, Lord, who hath believed our report? So then faith cometh by hearing, and hearing by the word of God.

1 PETER 3:17–22

For it is better, if the will of God be so, that ye suffer for well doing, than for evil doing. For Christ also hath once suffered for sins, the just for the unjust, that he might bring us to God, being put to death in the flesh, but quickened by the Spirit: By which also he went and preached unto the spirits in prison; Which sometime were disobedient, when once the longsuffering of God waited in the days of Noah, while the ark was a preparing, wherein few, that is, eight souls were saved by water. The like figure whereunto even baptism doth also now save us (not the putting away of the filth of the flesh, but the answer of a good conscience toward God,) by the resurrection of Jesus Christ: Who is gone into heaven, and is on the right hand of God; angels and authorities and powers being made subject unto him.

1 CORINTHIANS 12:12–13

For as the body is one, and hath many members, and all the members of that one body, being many, are one body: so also is Christ. For by one Spirit are we all baptized into one body, whether we be Jews or Gentiles, whether we be bond or free; and have been all made to drink into one Spirit.

So what does the bible say about baptism?

What is it?

Who is it for?

What does it do/symbolize?

How should it be carried out?

In our first reference in Mark 1, we have baptism and repentance, for the remission of sins. We see the crowds being baptized and confessing their sins.

The gospel itself uses God's law – the ten commandments – to reveal that we are all sinners and that we all need a

Saviour. This knowledge of our sin before a Holy God leads to a conviction – by the Holy Spirit – of our sin and genuine sorrow. This sorrow and realization of our eternal condition is what leads us to repentance, a turning away from our sin, our turning towards the Saviour, willingly receiving the payment Jesus made on the cross on our behalf and our faith in Him and his resurrection.

Acts 8 gives us the clearest example in scripture of this redemption. The Ethiopian eunuch is reading a copy of the scriptures and has Jesus's role explained to him by Philip. He then seeks baptism when they come across a body of water. He asks Philip if there is anything hindering his baptism and Philip replies that he may if he believes with his whole heart. The Ethiopian then confesses that he BELIEVES that Jesus is the Son of God and he and Philip go down INTO the water and Philip baptizes him. This passage shows us that baptism (in water) follows a profession of faith.

In Acts 16 Lydia, having her heart opened by the Lord – a working of the Holy Spirit – is baptized, along with her household. (No mention is made here of infants here so I believe there were not any in her household).

Later on in Acts 16 we see the jailer ask Paul what he must do to be saved and Paul tells him to believe on the Lord Jesus Christ (HAVE FAITH) and he will be saved. Paul further goes on to speak of the Word of the Lord (THE GOSPEL). The jailer and his whole house are baptized and sit down in the jailer's house and share a meal, believing in the Lord Jesus Christ.

Furthermore, in Acts 18, we see Crispus and his whole house believing and being baptized. In all these passages, we see no description of infants or small children being baptized. Whole household in this context would mean that there were nonesuch present. We cannot argue for infant baptism from absence in scripture.

All nations need to hear the gospel and those who believe need to be baptized. From these examples from the passages of Acts, we can understand baptism as an outward act of obedience – a symbol of an inward change – as commanded by Jesus. It is carried out after a profession of faith. A response to the gospel, that I understand as a conviction of sin, repentance from sin, a turning to Christ for the forgiveness from sin and exercising faith in Christ and his resurrection. These three are essential doctrines for Christian believers. Furthermore, Peter states in 1 Peter that baptism is the answer of a good conscience toward God.

The Holy Spirit came upon Jesus as he came up out of the water. The Gentiles received the Holy Spirit first and then were baptized. (Acts 19).

Believers receive the Holy Spirit when they come to Christ.

The word baptism itself comes from the Greek word βαπτίζω) "baptizo" meaning to immerse. It is found only in the New Testament, predominantly in the Book of Acts. The verb 'to sprinkle' in Greek is ῥαντίζω "rhantizo". The word 'to pour' is διαχέω "cheo". Neither are found in the New Testament in context to baptism.

Baptism is commanded by Jesus himself in Matthew 28, being one of only two commands or sacraments, the other being the Lord's Supper.

In Mark 1, Jesus comes up out of the water. Similarly, in Acts 37, Philip and the eunuch go down into the water for the baptism and then come up out of the water. This clearly infers that the eunuch was submerged into the water before then rising back out of the water, picturing Christ's death (falling back into the water), burial (being submerged underwater) and resurrection from the dead (rising out of the water).

Scripturally, baptism ALWAYS follows faith. Baptism without faith is meaningless. Indeed it's not baptism. Therefore baptism of babies or infants is unbiblical. How can a baby who cannot speak, have an understanding of their fallen state, or of their sin and be able to confess the Lord Jesus Christ as their saviour? Baptism in this case has no effect on the spiritual condition of the child.

Acts 2:39 states "For the promise is unto you, and to your children, and to all that are afar off, even as many as the Lord our God shall call."

Faith is a personal and individual response to the gospel, held by an individual. It cannot be held on one's behalf by someone else. There is no mention of god-parenting in scripture. We currently have a church full of baptized unbelievers – who may have been 'sprinkled' as babies – and unbaptized believers because of confusion on this issue.

Many would say that baptism is a secondary issue but I would state that there is a correct way to baptize and incorrect ways to baptize. The Anabaptists certainly thought it was a primary issue. Hundreds of them faced beheading or drowning in the 16th and 17th centuries in Germany for baptizing the way the bible commands. I even heard of a brother being thrown out of another brother's house when disagreement over baptism got heated!

What happens to unbaptized children if they die in childhood or before the age of accountability? I believe miscarried and stillborn children go to heaven because of God's grace.

Samuel 12:22-23: "And he said, While the child was yet alive, I fasted and wept: for I said, Who can tell whether GOD will be gracious to me, that the child may live? But now he is dead, wherefore should I fast? can I bring him back again? I shall go to him, but he shall not return to me."

I do not believe baptism is required for salvation, as salvation is by faith alone and we have the example of the thief on the cross. However, it is an act of obedience that we should seek to fulfil, if not straight after a profession of faith, then soon after. Why would you not obey his command if you truly love him and want to obey him?

In short, only people who have repented of their sin and have placed their trust in the Lord Jesus Christ i.e. confessed with their mouths, should be baptised.

Anglican Communion/Church of England (CoE)

Practices paedobaptism and credobaptism. Babies are 'sprinkled' or have their foreheads 'moistened'. Adults can have their heads rinsed over the font or opt for full immersion. But adults who were christened ('sprinkled') as babies cannot be baptized in church. They complete a confirmation course before they can receive the bread and the wine and become full members of the church. CoE considers adult baptism as re-baptism if the person seeking baptism were baptized as a baby, and hence won't do it. The church would understand the such a person as denying the validity of infant baptism and therefore the validity of paedobaptism itself.

Roman Catholicism/Orthodox

Practices paedobaptism and credobaptism. Believe baptism is required for salvation and is a way of attaining an initial state of grace.

Baptists

Practice credobaptism.

Methodists

Practice paedobaptism and credobaptism.

Climate Change

GENESIS 1

In the beginning God created the heaven and the earth.
And the earth was without form, and void; and darkness
was upon the face of the deep. And the Spirit of God
moved upon the face of the waters. And God said, Let
there be light: and there was light. And God saw the light,
that it was good: and God divided the light from the
darkness. And God called the light Day, and the darkness he
called Night. And the evening and the morning were the
first day. And God said, Let there be a firmament in the
midst of the waters, and let it divide the waters from the
waters. And God made the firmament, and divided the
waters which were under the firmament from the waters
which were above the firmament: and it was so. And God
called the firmament Heaven. And the evening and the
morning were the second day. And God said, Let the
waters under the heaven be gathered together unto one
place, and let the dry land appear: and it was so. And God
called the dry land Earth; and the gathering together of the
waters called he Seas: and God saw that it was good. And

God said, Let the earth bring forth grass, the herb yielding seed, and the fruit tree yielding fruit after his kind, whose seed is in itself, upon the earth: and it was so. And the earth brought forth grass, and herb yielding seed after his kind, and the tree yielding fruit, whose seed was in itself, after his kind: and God saw that it was good. And the evening and the morning were the third day. And God said, Let there be lights in the firmament of the heaven to divide the day from the night; and let them be for signs, and for seasons, and for days, and years: And let them be for lights in the firmament of the heaven to give light upon the earth: and it was so. And God made two great lights; the greater light to rule the day, and the lesser light to rule the night: he made the stars also. And God set them in the firmament of the heaven to give light upon the earth, And to rule over the day and over the night, and to divide the light from the darkness: and God saw that it was good. And the evening and the morning were the fourth day. And God said, Let the waters bring forth abundantly the moving creature that hath life, and fowl that may fly above the earth in the open firmament of heaven. And God created great whales, and every living creature that moveth, which the waters brought forth abundantly, after their kind, and every winged fowl after his kind: and God saw that it was good. And God blessed them, saying, Be fruitful, and multiply, and fill the waters in the seas, and let fowl multiply in the earth. And the evening and the morning were the fifth day. And God said, Let the earth bring forth the living creature after his kind, cattle, and creeping thing, and beast of the earth after his kind: and it was so. And God made the beast of the earth after his kind, and cattle after their kind, and every thing that creepeth upon the earth after his kind: and God saw that it was good. And God said, Let us make man in our image, after our likeness: and let them have dominion over the fish of the sea, and over the fowl of the air, and over the cattle, and over all the earth, and over every creeping thing that creepeth upon the earth. So God created man in his own image, in the image of God created he him; male and female created he them. And God blessed them, and God said unto them, Be fruitful, and multiply, and replenish the earth, and subdue it: and have dominion over the fish of the sea, and over the fowl of the air, and over every living thing that moveth upon the earth. And God said, Behold, I have given you every herb bearing seed, which is upon the face of all the earth, and every tree, in the which is the fruit of a tree yielding seed; to you it shall be for meat. And to every beast of the earth, and to every fowl of the air, and to every thing that creepeth upon the earth, wherein there is life, I have given every green herb for meat: and it was so. And God saw every thing that he had made, and, behold, it was very good. And the evening and the morning were the sixth day.

GENESIS 2:4-7

These are the generations of the heavens and of the earth when they were created, in the day that the LORD God made the earth and the heavens, And every plant of the field before it was in the earth, and every herb of the field before it grew: for the LORD God had not caused it to rain upon the earth, and there was not a man to till the ground. But there went up a mist from the earth, and watered the whole face of the ground. And the LORD God formed man of the dust of the ground, and breathed into his nostrils the breath of life; and man became a living soul.

GENESIS 5:1-5

This is the book of the generations of Adam. In the day that God created man, in the likeness of God made he him; Male and female created he them; and blessed them, and called their name Adam, in the day when they were created. And Adam lived an hundred and thirty years, and begat a son in his own likeness, after his image; and called his name Seth: And the days of Adam after he had begotten Seth were eight hundred years: and he begat sons and daughters: And all the days that Adam lived were nine hundred and thirty years: and he died.

GENESIS 5:25-27

And Methuselah lived an hundred eighty and seven years, and begat Lamech: And Methuselah lived after he begat Lamech seven hundred eighty and two years, and begat sons and daughters: And all the days of Methuselah were nine hundred sixty and nine
years: and he died.

GENESIS 7:1-5

And the LORD said unto Noah, Come thou and all thy house into the ark; for thee have I seen righteous before me in this generation. Of every clean beast thou shalt take to thee by sevens, the male and his female: and of beasts that are not clean by two, the male and his female. Of fowls also of the air by sevens, the male and the female; to keep seed alive upon the face of all the earth. For yet seven days, and I will cause it to rain upon the earth forty days and forty nights; and every living substance that I have made will I destroy from off the face of the earth. And Noah did according unto all that the LORD commanded him.

GENESIS 8:1–3, 16–22

And God remembered Noah, and every living thing, and all the cattle that was with him in the ark: and God made a wind to pass over the earth, and the waters asswaged;

The fountains also of the deep and the windows of heaven were stopped, and the rain from heaven was restrained;

And the waters returned from off the earth continually: and after the end of the hundred and fifty days the waters were abated... Go forth of the ark, thou, and thy wife, and thy sons, and thy sons' wives with thee. Bring forth with thee every living thing that is with thee, of all flesh, both of fowl, and of cattle, and of every creeping thing that creepeth upon the earth; that they may breed abundantly in the earth, and be fruitful, and multiply upon the earth. And Noah went forth, and his sons, and his wife, and his sons' wives with him: Every beast, every creeping thing, and every fowl, and whatsoever creepeth upon the earth, after their kinds, went forth out of the ark. And Noah builded an altar unto the LORD; and took of every clean beast, and of every clean fowl, and offered burnt offerings on the altar. And the LORD smelled a sweet savour; and the LORD said in his heart, I will not again curse the ground any more for man's sake; for the imagination of man's heart is evil from his youth; neither will I again smite any more every thing living, as I have done. While the earth remaineth, seedtime and harvest, and cold and heat, and summer and winter, and day and night shall not cease.

GENESIS 9:8–17

And God spake unto Noah, and to his sons with him, saying, And I, behold, I establish my covenant with you, and with your seed after you; And with every living creature that is with you, of the fowl, of the cattle, and of every beast of the earth with you; from all that go out of the ark, to every beast of the earth. And I will establish my covenant with you; neither shall all flesh be cut off any more by the waters of a flood; neither shall there any more be a flood to destroy the earth. And God said, This is the token of the covenant which I make between me and you and every living creature that is with you, for perpetual generations: I do set my bow in the cloud, and it shall be for a token of a covenant between me and the earth. And it shall come to pass, when I bring a cloud over the earth, that the bow shall be seen in the cloud: And I will remember my covenant, which is between me and you and every living creature of all flesh; and the waters shall no more become a flood to destroy all flesh. And the bow shall be in the cloud; and I will look upon it, that I may remember the everlasting covenant between God and every living creature of all flesh that is upon the earth. And God said unto Noah, This is the token of the covenant, which I have established between me and all flesh that is upon the earth.

EXODUS 20:11

For in six days the LORD made heaven and earth, the sea, and all that in them is, and rested the seventh day: wherefore the LORD blessed the sabbath day, and hallowed it.

DEUTRONOMY 28:12

The LORD shall open unto thee his good treasure, the heaven to give the rain unto thy land in his season, and to bless all the work of thine hand:

DEUTERONOMY 32:4

He is the Rock, his work is perfect: for all his ways are judgment: a God of truth and without iniquity, just and right is he.

JOB 38:1-11

Then the LORD answered Job out of the whirlwind, and said, Who is this that darkeneth counsel by words without knowledge? Gird up now thy loins like a man; for I will demand of thee, and answer thou me.

Where wast thou when I laid the foundations of the earth? declare, if thou hast understanding. Who hath laid the measures thereof, if thou knowest? or who hath stretched the line upon it? Whereupon are the foundations thereof fastened? or who laid the corner stone thereof; When the morning stars sang together, and all the sons of God shouted for joy? Or who shut up the sea with doors, when it brake forth, as if it had issued out of the womb? When I made the cloud the garment thereof, and thick darkness a swaddlingband for it, And brake up for it my decreed place, and set bars and doors, And said, Hitherto shalt thou come, but no further: and here shall thy proud waves be stayed?

PSALM 2:1–5

Why do the heathen rage, and the people imagine a vain thing? The kings of the earth set themselves, and the rulers take counsel together, against the LORD, and against his anointed, saying, Let us break their bands asunder, and cast away their cords from us. He that sitteth in the heavens shall laugh: the Lord shall have them in derision. Then shall he speak unto them in his wrath, and vex them in his sore displeasure.

PSALM 8:6–9

Thou madest him to have dominion over the works of thy hands; thou hast put all things under his feet: All sheep and oxen, yea, and the beasts of the field; The fowl of the air, and the fish of the sea, and whatsoever passeth through the paths of the seas. O LORD our Lord, how excellent is thy name in all the earth!

PSALM 24:1

A Psalm of David. The earth is the LORD'S, and the fulness thereof; the world, and they that dwell therein.

PSALM 19:1-9

(To the chief Musician, A Psalm of David}. The heavens declare the glory of God; and the firmament sheweth his handywork. Day unto day uttereth speech, and night unto night sheweth knowledge. There is no speech nor language, where their voice is not heard. Their line is gone out through all the earth, and their words to the end of the world. In them hath he set a tabernacle for the sun, Which is as a bridegroom coming out of his chamber, and rejoiceth as a strong man to run a race. His going forth is from the end of the heaven, and his circuit unto the ends of it: and there is nothing hid from the heat thereof. The law of the LORD is perfect, converting the soul: the testimony of the LORD is sure, making wise the simple. The statutes of the LORD are right, rejoicing the heart: the commandment of the LORD is pure, enlightening the eyes. The fear of the LORD is clean, enduring for ever: the judgments of the LORD are true and righteous altogether.

PSALM 46

{To the chief Musician for the sons of Korah, A Song upon Alamoth}. God is our refuge and strength, a very present help in trouble. Therefore will not we fear, though the earth be removed, and though the mountains be carried into the midst of the sea; Though the waters thereof roar and be troubled, though the mountains shake with the swelling thereof. Selah. There is a river, the streams whereof shall make glad the city of God, the holy place of the tabernacles of the most High.God is in the midst of her; she shall not be moved: God shall help her, and that right early. The heathen raged, the kingdoms were moved: he uttered his voice, the earth melted. The LORD of hosts is with us; the God of Jacob is our refuge. Selah. Come, behold the works of the LORD, what desolations he hath made in the earth. He maketh wars to cease unto the end of the earth; he breaketh the bow, and cutteth the spear in sunder; he burneth the chariot in the fire. Be still, and know that I am God: I will be exalted among the heathen, I will be exalted in the earth. The LORD of hosts is with us; the God of Jacob is our refuge. Selah.

PROVERBS 3:6

In all thy ways acknowledge him, and he shall direct thy paths.

ISAIAH 45:18-20

For thus saith the LORD that created the heavens; God himself that formed the earth and made it; he hath established it, he created it not in vain, he formed it to be inhabited: I am the LORD; and there is none else. I have not spoken in secret, in a dark place of the earth: I said not unto the seed of Jacob, Seek ye me in vain: I the LORD speak righteousness, I declare things that are right. Assemble yourselves and come; draw near together, ye that are escaped of the nations: they have no knowledge that set up the wood of their graven image, and pray unto a god that cannot save.

MATTHEW 5:45

That ye may be the children of your Father which is in heaven: for he maketh his sun to rise on the evil and on the good, and sendeth rain on the just and on the unjust.

MATTHEW 18:15–20

Moreover if thy brother shall trespass against thee, go and tell him his fault between thee and him alone: if he shall hear thee, thou hast gained thy brother. But if he will not hear thee, then take with thee one or two more, that in the mouth of two or three witnesses every word may be established. And if he shall neglect to hear them, tell it unto the church: but if he neglect to hear the church, let him be unto thee as an heathen man and a publican. Verily I say unto you, Whatsoever ye shall bind on earth shall be bound in heaven: and whatsoever ye shall loose on earth shall be loosed in heaven. Again I say unto you, That if two of you shall agree on earth as touching any thing that they shall ask, it shall be done for them of my Father which is in heaven. For where two or three are gathered together in my name, there am I in the midst of them.

MATTHEW 28:18-20

And Jesus came and spake unto them, saying, All power is given unto me in heaven and in earth. Go ye therefore, and teach all nations, baptizing them in the name of the Father, and of the Son, and of the Holy Ghost: Teaching them to observe all things whatsoever I have commanded you: and, lo, I am with you alway, even unto the end of the world. Amen.

ROMANS 8:28

And we know that all things work together for good to them that love God, to them who are the called according to his purpose.

1 CORINTHIANS 10:26

For the earth is the Lord's, and the fulness thereof.

PHILIPPIANS 4:4-7

Rejoice in the Lord alway: and again I say, Rejoice. Let your moderation be known unto all men. The Lord is at hand. Be careful for nothing; but in everything by prayer and supplication with thanksgiving let your requests be made known unto God. And the peace of God, which passeth all understanding, shall keep your hearts and minds through Christ Jesus.

HEBREWS 1:1-4

God, who at sundry times and in divers manners spake in time past unto the fathers by the prophets, Hath in these last days spoken unto us by his Son, whom he hath appointed heir of all things, by whom also he made the worlds; Who being the brightness of his glory, and the express image of his person, and upholding all things by the word of his power, when he had by himself purged our sins, sat down on the right hand of the Majesty on high; Being made so much better than the angels, as he hath by inheritance obtained a more excellent name than they.

HEBREWS 10:19–25

Having therefore, brethren, boldness to enter into the holiest by the blood of Jesus, By a new and living way, which he hath consecrated for us, through the veil, that is to say, his flesh; And having an high priest over the house of God; Let us draw near with a true heart in full assurance of faith, having our hearts sprinkled from an evil conscience, and our bodies washed with pure water. Let us hold fast the profession of our faith without wavering; (for he is faithful that promised;) And let us consider one another to provoke unto love and to good works: Not forsaking the assembling of ourselves together, as the manner of some is; but exhorting one another: and so much the more, as ye see the day approaching.

HEBREWS 12:1–3

Wherefore seeing we also are compassed about with so great a cloud of witnesses, let us lay aside every weight, and the sin which doth so easily beset us, and let us run with patience the race that is set before us, Looking unto Jesus the author and finisher of our faith; who for the joy that was set before him endured the cross, despising the shame, and is set down at the right hand of the throne of God. For consider him that endured such contradiction of sinners against himself, lest ye be wearied and faint in your minds.

2 TIMOTHY 1:3-10

I thank God, whom I serve from my forefathers with pure conscience, that without ceasing I have remembrance of thee in my prayers night and day; Greatly desiring to see thee, being mindful of thy tears, that I may be filled with joy; When I call to remembrance the unfeigned faith that is in thee, which dwelt first in thy grandmother Lois, and thy mother Eunice; and I am persuaded that in thee also. Wherefore I put thee in remembrance that thou stir up the gift of God, which is in thee by the putting on of my hands. For God hath not given us the spirit of fear; but of power, and of love, and of a sound mind. Be not thou therefore ashamed of the testimony of our Lord, nor of me his prisoner: but be thou partaker of the afflictions of the gospel according to the power of God; Who hath saved us, and called us with an holy calling, not according to our works, but according to his own purpose and grace, which was given us in Christ Jesus before the world began, But is now made manifest by the appearing of our Saviour Jesus Christ, who hath abolished death, and hath brought life and immortality to light through the gospel:

1 PETER 5:6-7

Humble yourselves therefore under the mighty hand of God, that he may exalt you in due time: Casting all your care upon him; for he careth for you.

2 PETER 3:5-6

For this they willingly are ignorant of, that by the word of God the heavens were of old, and the earth standing out of the water and in the water: Whereby the world that then was, being overflowed with water, perished: But the heavens and the earth, which are now, by the same word are kept in store, reserved unto fire against the day of judgment and perdition of ungodly men.

1 JOHN 4:15-21

Whosoever shall confess that Jesus is the Son of God, God dwelleth in him, and he in God. And we have known and believed the love that God hath to us. God is love; and he that dwelleth in love dwelleth in God, and God in him. Herein is our love made perfect, that we may have boldness in the day of judgment: because as he is, so are we in this world. There is no fear in love; but perfect love casteth out fear: because fear hath torment. He that feareth is not made perfect in love. We love him, because he first loved us. If a man say, I love God, and hateth his brother, he is a liar: for he that loveth not his brother whom he hath seen, how can he love God whom he hath not seen? And this commandment have we from him, That he who loveth God love his brother also.

REVELATION 21

And I saw a new heaven and a new earth: for the first heaven and the first earth were passed away; and there was no more sea. And I John saw the holy city, new Jerusalem, coming down from God out of heaven, prepared as a bride adorned for her husband. And I heard a great voice out of heaven saying, Behold, the tabernacle of God is with men, and he will dwell with them, and they shall be his people, and God himself shall be with them, and be their God. And God shall wipe away all tears from their eyes; and there shall be no more death, neither sorrow, nor crying, neither shall there be any more pain: for the former things are passed away. And he that sat upon the throne said, Behold, I make all things new. And he said unto me, Write: for these words are true and faithful. And he said unto me, It is done. I am Alpha and Omega, the beginning and the end. I will give unto him that is athirst of the fountain of the water of life freely. He that overcometh shall inherit all things; and I will be his God, and he shall be my son. But the fearful, and unbelieving, and the abominable, and murderers, and whoremongers, and sorcerers, and idolaters, and all liars, shall have their part in the lake which burneth with fire and brimstone: which is the second death. And there came unto me one of the seven angels which had the seven vials full of the seven last plagues, and talked with me, saying, Come hither, I will shew thee the bride, the Lamb's wife. And he carried me away in the spirit to a great and high mountain, and shewed me that great city, the holy Jerusalem, descending out of heaven from God, Having the glory of God: and her light was like unto a stone most precious, even like a jasper stone, clear as crystal; And had a wall great and high, and had twelve gates, and at the gates twelve angels, and names written thereon, which are the names of the twelve tribes of the children of Israel: On the east three gates; on the north three gates; on the south three gates; and on the west three gates. And the wall of the city had twelve foundations, and in them the names of the twelve apostles of the Lamb. And he that talked with me had a golden reed to measure the city, and the gates thereof, and the wall thereof. And the city lieth foursquare, and the length is as large as the breadth: and he measured the city with the reed, twelve thousand furlongs. The length and the breadth and the height of it are equal. And he measured the wall thereof, an hundred and forty and four cubits, according to the measure of a man, that is, of the angel. And the building of the wall of it was of jasper: and the city was pure gold, like unto clear glass. And the foundations of the wall of the city were garnished with all manner of precious stones. The first foundation was jasper; the second, sapphire; the third, a chalcedony; the fourth, an emerald; The fifth, sardonyx; the sixth, sardius; the seventh, chrysolite; the eighth, beryl; the ninth, a topaz; the tenth, a chrysoprasus; the eleventh, a jacinth; the twelfth, an amethyst. And the twelve gates were twelve pearls; every several gate was of one pearl: and the street of the city was pure gold, as it were transparent glass. And I saw no temple therein: for the Lord God Almighty and the Lamb are the temple of it. And the city had no need of the sun, neither of the moon, to shine in it: for the glory of God did lighten it, and the Lamb is the light thereof. And the nations of them which are saved shall walk in the light of it: and the kings of the earth do bring their glory and honour into it. And the gates of it shall not be shut at all by day: for there shall be no night there. And they shall bring the glory and honour of the nations into it. And there shall in no wise enter into it any thing that defileth, neither whatsoever worketh abomination, or maketh a lie: but they which are written in the Lamb's book of life.

REVELATION 22:1–5

And he shewed me a pure river of water of life, clear as crystal, proceeding out of the throne of God and of the Lamb. In the midst of the street of it, and on either side of the river, was there the tree of life, which bare twelve manner of fruits, and yielded her fruit every month: and the leaves of the tree were for the healing of the nations. And there shall be no more curse: but the throne of God and of the Lamb shall be in it; and his servants shall serve him: And they shall see his face; and his name shall be in their foreheads. And there shall be no night there; and they need no candle, neither light of the sun; for the Lord God giveth them light: and they shall reign for ever and ever.

In this chapter we will examine what is probably the issue of our present time – I'm writing this in 2022/2023 – namely climate change, which was formally known as global warming. To many it is a settled issue and those who disagree with this orthodoxy are dismissed as sceptics or even worse, climate change deniers (with all the connotations that entails).

Essentially the idea is that mankind is entirely responsible for the current increase in average global temperatures, a direct result of CO_2 being emitted as we go about our lives, and that if we don't reduce our CO_2 emissions the planet will heat up, to a point where no human and animal life will survive, i.e. we will face a mass extinction event.

Whilst discussing this topic I will endeavour to answer these questions:

Is climate change happening?

Need we be worried?

Where is God in this?

The book of Genesis is so important to understand what is going on in the world today and the first passage of Genesis 1 is our starting point. We learn that God is the creator of all things:

"In the beginning (TIME), God created the heaven (SPACE) and the earth (MATTER)".

For God to be able to do this, he must be outside of all three, otherwise he would be dependent on one or all of them and hence wouldn't be God. Time, space and matter have to be created in that order, as matter has to have a space in which to be put, and time has to exist for this action to happen at some point. Also note in this verse that the King James Version correctly translates 'heaven' instead of 'heavens' as the newer versions translate it. The firmament (heaven) – singular – is initially created as one space but is later divided up into three:

The firmament under heaven – the sky (Genesis 1:20) and the firmament in which the stars are found – outer space (Genesis 1:14-18), and the third heaven – where God is (2 Corinthians 2:12).

Furthermore, the passage from Isaiah 45 tells us that God created the earth to be inhabited. Genesis 1 gives us a day-by-day description of what God did and the steps he took to create a perfect creation. God created everything seen and unseen from nothing! We learn also that God gives mankind dominion over all the Earth, and all the animals and creatures therein. We are responsible for it all.

But we live in a fallen world because of Adam's sin. The world is no longer perfect, and all of mankind has inherited Adam's sin nature as we are all his descendants.

Currently, Earth's landmasses make up 30% of its surface area, with only 3% of said landmasses habitable for mankind. The Earth we observe today is clearly not the same as the planet God created, as the list of Adam's descendants to Noah in Genesis 5 tells us that humans once lived to be over nine hundred years old!

God created the earth, the moon, the sun and the stars; all the chemical elements, space and time. He is also responsible for all the laws that govern his creation. He upholds it all through the power of his word:

"Who being the brightness of his glory, and the express image of his person, and upholding all things by the word of his power." Hebrews 1:3.

The flood account in Genesis 7 tells us that God is in control of the weather. The passages from Deuteronomy 28 and Matthew 5:45 confirm this. So even though we all understand the water cycle of precipitation and evaporation, it is God who controls it. Interestingly, God tells Noah to COME into the ark in Genesis 7:1. God was in the ark with Noah, and it was the Lord himself who shut Noah in:

"And they that went in, went in male and female of all flesh, as God had commanded him: and the LORD shut him in." Genesis 7:16.

"And every living substance was destroyed which was upon the face of the ground, both man, and cattle, and the creeping things, and the fowl of the heaven; and they were destroyed from the earth: and Noah only remained alive, and they that were with him in the ark." Genesis 7:23.

God commanded (caused) the rain to fall to wipe out all of mankind except for Noah and his family and the creatures in the ark.

After the floodwaters had receded, Noah and his family exit the ark and God makes a covenant with them. He promises to never again send a (global) flood to destroy the world, (humans and animals). He sets a rainbow in the clouds as a visual sign of this covenant, as a constant reminder for all to look upon it and remember. I wonder how many people today look upon a rainbow and remember Noah's flood and God's covenant.

The passage from Job tells us that God sets the boundaries of the seas and how far the waves are allowed to travel. He does allow tidal waves as a result of earthquakes, but not a global flood. It seems but we humans do not comprehend all of his ways.

The air we breathe is made up of 75% nitrogen and 24% oxygen. The remaining 1% is made up of trace gases. CO_2 is 0.06%. Of this 0.06%, 97% of CO_2 emissions are from natural sources e.g. volcanic activity, animal activity etc. and only 3% is directly from human activity according to the IPCC. And of that 3%, the United Kingdom, for example, is responsible for 1%. And 1% of 3% of 0.06% is a miniscule amount, namely 0.00000018%. The fact is we need CO_2. Plants take it in and convert it into food and give out oxygen that humans need to breathe. At CO_2 levels of 200ppm plant life ceases to grow and at 150ppm they start to die.

Environmentalism has become an Idol, a god to be worshipped. We ought to worship the creator not the creation. Al Gore is wrong! The 'science' that mankind is responsible for climate change is not settled. Not by a country mile. Indeed, the climate has been changing since Noah's flood. There have been periods of cooling and periods of warming. The Roman warm period allowed grapes to be grown in Yorkshire! The colder Dark Ages followed, which in turn were followed by the medieval warm period. A period of prolonged cooling followed and was known as the 'Little Ice Age', which lasted into the middle of the nineteenth century. There has been gradual warming up to the present day. Some scientists expect Europe to enter a period of cooling.

"For this they willingly are ignorant of, that by the word of God the heavens were of old, and the earth standing out of the water and in the water: Whereby the world that then was, being overflowed with water, perished: But the heavens and the earth, which are now, by the same word are kept in store, reserved unto fire against the day of judgment and perdition of ungodly men."

This passage from 2 Peter 3 tells us that people are willingly ignorant of the creation, the flood and the coming judgment: the creation – that God created everything and therefore gets to make the rules; the flood – that God can judge his creation and destroy it if he so chooses; the coming judgement – that God will one day judge everyone, the living and the dead.

God will ultimately destroy the earth when he creates a new heaven and new earth. He will not allow mankind to destroy the planet. Genesis 8:22 tells us that whilst the earth exists, the weather and seasons will continue.

Christians really have nothing to fear: God is with us by the indwelling of the Holy Spirit, and the Bible lays out what will happen in the end. Once one abandons the truth of scripture, one is susceptible to all kinds of falsehood and worry. The Bible has numerous passages exhorting believers not to worry about anything. Philippians 4:4-7 for example speaks so strongly and clearly into this:

"Rejoice in the Lord alway: and again I say, Rejoice. Let your moderation be known unto all men. The Lord is at hand. Be careful for nothing; but in everything by prayer and supplication with thanksgiving let your requests be made known unto God. And the peace of God, which passeth all understanding, shall keep your hearts and minds through Christ Jesus."

The climate changes. It has done since Noah's flood. And it will continue to do so until God creates a new heaven and a new Earth. Mankind may or may not have an effect on the climate. God is with us. We need not worry.

There are certain powers in the world that want to have mankind in a perpetual stage of worry and fear. We ought to fear God! Trust in him, pray and ask for his comfort, and be anxious about nothing. Have faith!

In short, we don't need to worry about climate change as God is in control of everything.

The majority of denominations in the UK subscribe to the idea of anthropomorphic climate change.

Death Penalty

GENESIS 9:6

Whoso sheddeth man's blood, by man shall his blood be shed: for in the image of God made he man.

EXODUS 20:13

Thou shalt not kill.

EXODUS 21:22–25

If men strive, and hurt a woman with child, so that her fruit depart from her, and yet no mischief follow: he shall be surely punished, according as the woman's husband will lay upon him; and he shall pay as the judges determine. And if any mischief follow, then thou shalt give life for life, Eye for eye, tooth for tooth, hand for hand, foot for foot, Burning for burning, wound for wound, stripe for stripe.

EXODUS 31:12–17

And the LORD spake unto Moses, saying, Speak thou also unto the children of Israel, saying, Verily my sabbaths ye shall keep: for it is a sign between me and you throughout your generations; that ye may know that I am the LORD that doth sanctify you. Ye shall keep the sabbath therefore; for it is holy unto you: every one that defileth it shall surely be put to death: for whosoever doeth any work therein, that soul shall be cut off from among his people. Six days may work be done; but in the seventh is the sabbath of rest, holy to the LORD: whosoever doeth any work in the sabbath day, he shall surely be put to death. Wherefore the children of Israel shall keep the sabbath, to observe the sabbath throughout their generations, for a perpetual covenant. It is a sign between me and the children of Israel for ever: for in six days the LORD made heaven and earth, and on the seventh day he rested, and was refreshed.

LEVITICUS 20:1-5

And the LORD spake unto Moses, saying, Again, thou shalt say to the children of Israel, Whosoever he be of the children of Israel, or of the strangers that sojourn in Israel, that giveth any of his seed unto Molech; he shall surely be put to death: the people of the land shall stone him with stones. And I will set my face against that man, and will cut him off from among his people; because he hath given of his seed unto Molech, to defile my sanctuary, and to profane my holy name. And if the people of the land do any ways hide their eyes from the man, when he giveth of his seed unto Molech, and kill him not: Then I will set my face against that man, and against his family, and will cut him off, and all that go a whoring after him, to commit whoredom with Molech, from among their people.

LEVITICUS 20:9

For every one that curseth his father or his mother shall be surely put to death: he hath cursed his father or his mother; his blood shall be upon him.

NUMBERS 35:6–34

And among the cities which ye shall give unto the Levites there shall be six cities for refuge, which ye shall appoint for the manslayer, that he may flee thither: and to them ye shall add forty and two cities. So all the cities which ye shall give to the Levites shall be forty and eight cities: them shall ye give with their suburbs. And the cities which ye shall give shall be of the possession of the children of Israel: from them that have many ye shall give many; but from them that have few ye shall give few: every one shall give of his cities unto the Levites according to his inheritance which he inheriteth. And the LORD spake unto Moses, saying, Speak unto the children of Israel, and say unto them, When ye be come over Jordan into the land of Canaan; Then ye shall appoint you cities to be cities of refuge for you; that the slayer may flee thither, which killeth any person at unawares. And they shall be unto you cities for refuge from the avenger; that the manslayer die not, until he stand before the congregation in judgment. And of these cities which ye shall give six cities shall ye have for refuge. Ye shall give three cities on this side Jordan, and three cities shall ye give in the land of Canaan, which shall be cities of refuge. These six cities shall be a refuge, both for the children of Israel, and for the stranger, and for the sojourner among them: that every one that killeth any person unawares may flee thither. And if he smite him with an instrument of iron, so that he die, he is a murderer: the murderer shall surely be put to death. And if he smite him with throwing a stone, wherewith he may die, and he die, he is a murderer: the murderer shall surely be put to death. Or if he smite him with an hand weapon of wood, wherewith he may die, and he die, he is a murderer: the murderer shall surely be put to death. The revenger of blood himself shall slay the murderer: when he meeteth him, he shall slay him. But if he thrust him of hatred, or hurl at him by laying of wait, that he die; Or in enmity smite him with his hand, that he die: he that smote him shall surely be put to death; for he is a murderer: the revenger of blood shall slay the murderer, when he meeteth him. But if he thrust him suddenly without enmity, or have cast upon him any thing without laying of wait, Or with any stone, wherewith a man may die, seeing him not, and cast it upon him, that he die, and was not his enemy, neither sought his harm: Then the congregation shall judge between the slayer and the revenger of blood according to these judgments: And the congregation shall deliver the slayer out of the hand of the revenger of blood, and the congregation shall restore him to the city of his refuge, whither he was fled: and he shall abide in it unto the death of the high priest, which was anointed with the holy oil. But if the slayer shall at any time come without the border of the city of his refuge, whither he was fled; And the revenger of blood find him without the borders of the city of his refuge, and the revenger of blood kill the slayer; he shall not be guilty of blood: Because he should have remained in the city of his refuge until the death of the high priest: but after the death of the high priest the slayer shall return into the land of his possession. So these things shall be for a statute of judgment unto you throughout your generations in all your dwellings. Whoso killeth any person, the murderer shall be put to death by the mouth of witnesses: but one witness shall not testify against any person to cause him to die. Moreover ye shall take no satisfaction for the life of a murderer, which is guilty of death: but he shall be surely put to death. And ye shall take no satisfaction for him that is fled to the city of his refuge, that he should come again to dwell in the land, until the death of the priest. So ye shall not pollute the land wherein ye are: for blood it defileth the land: and the land cannot be cleansed of the blood that is shed therein, but by the blood of him that shed it. Defile not therefore the land which ye shall inhabit, wherein I dwell: for I the LORD dwell among the children of Israel.

DEUTERONOMY 4:41–43

Then Moses severed three cities on this side Jordan toward the sunrising; That the slayer might flee thither, which should kill his neighbour unawares, and hated him not in times past; and that fleeing unto one of these cities he might live: Namely, Bezer in the wilderness, in the plain country, of the Reubenites; and Ramoth in Gilead, of the Gadites; and Golan in Bashan, of the Manassites.

DEUTERONOMY 5:17

Thou shalt not kill.

DEUTERONOMY 17:2–7

If there be found among you, within any of thy gates which the LORD thy God giveth thee, man or woman, that hath wrought wickedness in the sight of the LORD thy God, in transgressing his covenant, And hath gone and served other gods, and worshipped them, either the sun, or moon, or any of the host of heaven, which I have not commanded; And it be told thee, and thou hast heard of it, and inquired diligently, and, behold, it be true, and the thing certain, that such abomination is wrought in Israel: Then shalt thou bring forth that man or that woman, which have committed that wicked thing, unto thy gates, even that man or that woman, and shalt stone them with stones, till they die. At the mouth of two witnesses, or three witnesses, shall he that is worthy of death be put to death; but at the mouth of one witness he shall not be put to death. The hands of the witnesses shall be first upon him to put him to death, and afterward the hands of all the people. So thou shalt put the evil away from among you.

DEUTERONOMY 19:1–7

When the LORD thy God hath cut off the nations, whose land the LORD thy God giveth thee, and thou succeedest them, and dwellest in their cities, and in their houses; Thou shalt separate three cities for thee in the midst of thy land, which the LORD thy God giveth thee to possess it. Thou shalt prepare thee a way, and divide the coasts of thy land, which the LORD thy God giveth thee to inherit, into three parts, that every slayer may flee thither. And this is the case of the slayer, which shall flee thither, that he may live: Whoso killeth his neighbour ignorantly, whom he hated not in time past; As when a man goeth into the wood with his neighbour to hew wood, and his hand fetcheth a stroke with the axe to cut down the tree, and the head slippeth from the helve, and lighteth upon his neighbour, that he die; he shall flee unto one of those cities, and live: Lest the avenger of the blood pursue the slayer, while his heart is hot, and overtake him, because the way is long, and slay him; whereas he was not worthy of death, inasmuch as he hated him not in time past. Wherefore I command thee, saying, Thou shalt separate three cities for thee.

DEUTERONOMY 19:11-13

But if any man hate his neighbour, and lie in wait for him, and rise up against him, and smite him mortally that he die, and fleeth into one of these cities: Then the elders of his city shall send and fetch him thence, and deliver him into the hand of the avenger of blood, that he may die. Thine eye shall not pity him, but thou shalt put away the guilt of innocent blood from Israel, that it may go well with thee.

DEUTERONOMY 19:15-21

One witness shall not rise up against a man for any iniquity, or for any sin, in any sin that he sinneth: at the mouth of two witnesses, or at the mouth of three witnesses, shall the matter be established. If a false witness rise up against any man to testify against him that which is wrong; Then both the men, between whom the controversy is, shall stand before the LORD, before the priests and the judges, which shall be in those days; And the judges shall make diligent inquisition: and, behold, if the witness be a false witness, and hath testified falsely against his brother; Then shall ye do unto him, as he had thought to have done unto his brother: so shalt thou put the evil away from among you. And those which remain shall hear, and fear, and shall henceforth commit no more any such evil among you. And thine eye shall not pity; but life shall go for life, eye for eye, tooth for tooth, hand for hand, foot for foot.

DEUTERONOMY 21:18–21

If a man have a stubborn and rebellious son, which will not obey the voice of his father, or the voice of his mother, and that, when they have chastened him, will not hearken unto them: Then shall his father and his mother lay hold on him, and bring him out unto the elders of his city, and unto the gate of his place; And they shall say unto the elders of his city, This our on is stubborn and rebellious, he will not obey our voice; he is a glutton, and a drunkard. And all the men of his city shall stone him with stones, that he die: so shalt thou put evil away from among you; and all Israel shall hear, and fear.

DEUTERONOMY 32:4

He is the Rock, his work is perfect: for all his ways are judgment: a God of truth and without iniquity, just and right is he.

DEUTERONOMY 32:35-36

To me belongeth vengeance, and recompence; their foot shall slide in due time: for the day of their calamity is at hand, and the things that shall come upon them make haste. For the LORD shall judge his people, and repent himself for his servants, when he seeth that their power is gone, and there is none shut up, or left.

PSALM 19:1-9

{To the chief Musician, A Psalm of David}. The heavens declare the glory of God; and the firmament sheweth his handywork. Day unto day uttereth speech, and night unto night sheweth knowledge. There is no speech nor language, where their voice is not heard. Their line is gone out through all the earth, and their words to the end of the world. In them hath he set a tabernacle for the sun, Which is as a bridegroom coming out of his chamber, and rejoiceth as a strong man to run a race. His going forth is from the end of the heaven, and his circuit unto the ends of it: and there is nothing hid from the heat thereof. The law of the LORD is perfect, converting the soul: the testimony of the LORD is sure, making wise the simple. The statutes of the LORD are right, rejoicing the heart: the commandment of the LORD is pure, enlightening the eyes. The fear of the LORD is clean, enduring for ever: the judgments of the LORD are true and righteous altogether.

MATTHEW 5:38-39

Ye have heard that it hath been said, An eye for an eye, and a tooth for a tooth: But I say unto you, That ye resist not evil: but whosoever shall smite thee on thy right cheek, turn to him the other also.

MATTHEW 18:15-18

Moreover if thy brother shall trespass against thee, go and tell him his fault between thee and him alone: if he shall hear thee, thou hast gained thy brother. But if he will not hear thee, then take with thee one or two more, that in the mouth of two or three witnesses every word may be established. And if he shall neglect to hear them, tell it unto the church: but if he neglect to hear the church, let him be unto thee as an heathen man and a publican. Verily I say unto you, Whatsoever ye shall bind on earth shall be bound in heaven: and whatsoever ye shall loose on earth shall be loosed in heaven.

MATTHEW 26:51–52
And, behold, one of them which were with Jesus stretched out his hand, and drew his sword, and struck a servant of the high priest's, and smote off his ear. Then said Jesus unto him, Put up again thy sword into his place: for all they that take the sword shall perish with the sword.

JOHN 8:1–11
Jesus went unto the mount of Olives. And early in the morning he came again into the temple, and all the people came unto him; and he sat down, and taught them. And the scribes and Pharisees brought unto him a woman taken in adultery; and when they had set her in the midst, They say unto him, Master, this woman was taken in adultery, in the very act. Now Moses in the law commanded us, that such should be stoned: but what sayest thou? This they said, tempting him, that they might have to accuse him. But Jesus stooped down, and with his finger wrote on the ground, as though he heard them not. So when they

continued asking him, he lifted up himself, and said unto them, He that is without sin among you, let him first cast a stone at her. And again he stooped down, and wrote on the ground. And they which heard it, being convicted by their own conscience, went out one by one, beginning at the eldest, even unto the last: and Jesus was left alone, and the woman standing in the midst. When Jesus had lifted up himself, and saw none but the woman, he said unto her, Woman, where are those thine accusers? hath no man condemned thee? She said, No man, Lord. And Jesus said unto her, Neither do I condemn thee: go, and sin no more.

ROMANS 12:14-21

Bless them which persecute you: bless, and curse not. Rejoice with them that do rejoice, and weep with them that weep. Be of the same mind one toward another. Mind not high things, but condescend to men of low estate. Be not wise in your own conceits. Recompense to no man evil for evil. Provide things honest in the sight of all men. If it be possible, as much as lieth in you, live peaceably with all men. Dearly beloved, avenge not yourselves, but rather give place unto wrath: for it is written, Vengeance is mine; I will repay, saith the Lord. Therefore if thine enemy hunger, feed him; if he thirst, give him drink: for in so doing thou shalt heap coals of fire on his head. Be not overcome of evil, but overcome evil with good.

ROMANS 13:1–10

Let every soul be subject unto the higher powers. For there is no power but of God: the powers that be are ordained of God. Whosoever therefore resisteth the power, resisteth the ordinance of God: and they that resist shall receive to themselves damnation. For rulers are not a terror to good works, but to the evil. Wilt thou then not be afraid of the power? do that which is good, and thou shalt have praise of the same: For he is the minister of God to thee for good. But if thou do that which is evil, be afraid; for he beareth not the sword in vain: for he is the minister of God, a revenger to execute wrath upon him that doeth evil. Therefore ye must needs be subject, not only for wrath, but also for conscience sake. For for this cause pay ye tribute also: for they are God's ministers, attending continually upon this very thing. Render therefore to all their dues: tribute to whom tribute is due; custom to whom custom; fear to whom fear; honour to whom honour. Owe no man any thing, but to love one another: for he that loveth another hath fulfilled the law. For this, Thou shalt not commit adultery, Thou shalt not kill, Thou shalt not steal, Thou shalt not bear false witness, Thou shalt not covet; and if there be any other commandment, it is briefly comprehended in this saying, namely, Thou shalt love thy neighbour as thyself. Love worketh no ill to his neighbour: therefore love is the fulfilling of the law.

EPHESIANS 6:1–4

Children, obey your parents in the Lord: for this is right. Honour thy father and mother; (which is the first commandment with promise;) That it may be well with thee, and thou mayest live long on the earth. And, ye fathers, provoke not your children to wrath: but bring them up in the nurture and admonition of the Lord.

2 CORINTHIANS 13-1:4

This is the third time I am coming to you. In the mouth of two or three witnesses shall every word be established. I told you before, and foretell you, as if I were present, the second time; and being absent now I write to them which heretofore have sinned, and to all other, that, if I come again, I will not spare: Since ye seek a proof of Christ speaking in me, which to you-ward is not weak, but is mighty in you. For though he was crucified through weakness, yet he liveth by the power of God. For we also are weak in him, but we shall live with him by the power of God toward you.

HEBREWS 10:30–31

For we know him that hath said, Vengeance belongeth unto me, I will recompense, saith the Lord. And again, The Lord shall judge his people. It is a fearful thing to fall into the hands of the living God.

Does the Bible condone the death penalty?

Should it apply to today?

God himself institutes the death penalty in Genesis. It is a principle that applies to all mankind. As such, it is part of the earliest moral law, given to Noah after the flood. In principle it is an example of restorative justice, where punishment matches the crime. For example: a life for a life. It is repeated in Exodus 20 and then expounded in Exodus 21 and Leviticus 20. As we saw in the Abortion chapter, Exodus 21 states that causing an injury to the mother and/or her unborn child could result in the use of the death penalty. Exodus 31 commands the death penalty for anyone breaking the Sabbath.

God takes the welfare of the unborn and of children very seriously as we can see in Leviticus 20, where we read that anyone sacrificing their children to Molech (literally burning them to death) is to be put to death by stoning. This is our first reference to the manner of execution in the Bible. In this passage the consequence for not executing the guilty is that God himself will 'cut them off', them, their family and all who 'go a whoring after Molech' i.e. God will kill them.

Numbers 35 repeats that murderers are to be executed but adds that there must be witnesses, one witness being insufficient for the death penalty to be carried out. This passage is also our first mention of a city of refuge, where one suspected of murder is to flee to and reside in until the death of the priest. At which point he can return to the land from whence he fled. We also learn that the 'shedding of blood' – that is to say murder – defiles the land, and the land can only be cleansed by the blood of the one who shed it. Here it appears to indicate that it morally pollutes the land not to execute murderers.

The Old Testament book of Deuteronomy has the most to say about the death penalty, starting by reiterating the command not to kill. (Deuteronomy 5).

Deuteronomy 17 institutes the death penalty by stoning for any man or woman in the land breaking the covenant, by worshipping other gods or the sun, moon or stars, after diligent inquiries and at the mouth of two or three witnesses. Once again a single witness is insufficient. Further, the witnesses had to throw the first stones. The idea of two or three witnesses is picked up again in Matthew 18:

"...that in the mouth of two or three witnesses every word may be established."

So far, we see that God commands us not to kill and that a murderer is to be executed by stoning. Committing idolatry also carries the death penalty. Now looking at

Deuteronomy 19, we learn that killing someone with malice aforethought – known to us as murder – carries the death penalty. In the passage the murderer flees to a city of refuge, but the elders of the city get him back and execute him and, in doing so, put away the guilt of the innocent blood from Israel, cleansing the sin from the land, "that it may go well with thee". In that way God will continue to bless the land and the people. There is a real necessity to carry out justice and not allow unpunished sin to pollute the land.

Deuteronomy 19 also gives us an example of killing by accident – that we would call manslaughter – with the guilty party fleeing to a city of refuge so that they are not killed in retribution, which would be an unlawful killing. The Bible here is telling us that manslaughter does not carry the death penalty.

Deuteronomy 19 continues and reiterates the requirement for two or three witnesses but further requires the witness not to have committed the same sin as the person against whom they testify. Someone found guilty of giving false witness is to be punished in the same manner as they sought to have had done to the one accused. The fear of this punishment is to act as a deterrent against giving false witness, and the guilty party is not to pitied.

Deuteronomy 21 permits the death penalty for repeated and rebellious disobedience towards one's parents and being a threat to the society, in drunkenness and gluttony. Disobedience to one's parents is disobedience to God (see Ephesians 6.)

The principle of first mention shows us how God feels about a certain issue and how it is to be dealt with. We should therefore take note of the first time a subject is recorded in scripture. God does not always respond the same on subsequent occasions. There is space for his mercy and grace. We see this with King David and his adultery with Bathsheba (and the murder of her husband.) King David should have been executed but instead God had mercy on him and called him to repentance using the prophet Nathan.

Deuteronomy 32 and Psalm 19 tell us that God's law is perfect; that God is just and right, and that his judgements are true and righteous. This would mean that the death penalty (as laid out in the Old Testament and carried out in accordance to the guidance given therein) is also right and just.

In the Old Testament, God shows us how a nation should function, as a model nation. Many of the principles involved are carried forward into the New Testament.

In Matthew 5, "eye for an eye" is expanded to include the command to "turn the other cheek." When considered with the OT this seems to be a rule between individuals. One is not to seek vengeance against another, but this does not negate the state or ruler's authority and responsibility to carry out punishment of evildoers, including the death penalty.

Matthew 18 repeats the requirement found in the Old Testament for two or three witnesses, in order for the truth to be established. Matthew 26 contains the oft-quoted verse of "He who lives by the sword shall die by the sword", rendered in the King James as "for all they that take the sword shall perish with the sword."

The principle of "Eye for an eye...", once again being applied and Jesus here seeming to uphold the death penalty.

The passage from John 8 is our key text on this topic. We have a clear case of adultery having been committed for which the punishment is death – which would have been carried out after a trial with two or three witnesses as we have established. The Pharisees are, of course, attempting to trick Jesus but their plan backfires on them. First of all, where is the man who was involved? The Old Testament law required both parties to the adultery to be taken. It was hypocritical to bring just the women.

Jesus's point that "He that is without sin among you, let him first cast a stone at her" is interesting. He isn't demanding that only sinless people can carry out the death penalty – in which, case no one could do the stoning as only he is sinless – rather he is reiterating the requirement that only people who have not committed the same sin as the one accused can stand in judgement. Perhaps that is what he was writing on the ground – the details of the Pharisees and their adulteries i.e. he is exposing their hypocrisy. They depart, one by one, leaving only Jesus and the woman. With no witnesses the trial cannot go ahead so Jesus dismisses her case and sends her on her way, telling her to go and sin no more, to stop committing adultery.

Romans 12 reiterates that Christians are not to seek vengeance themselves but allow God to do it, repeating what is said in Deuteronomy 32. Romans 13 tells us that the people who rule over us are a terror to evil works, of whom we should fear, for they bear not the sword in vain – that they have the authority to punish evil, being ministers (servants) of God. The Bible here clearly seems to say the Christians are to relinquish the authority for punishing evil to their rulers who God has appointed and uses to carry out punishment. It does not say that rulers and authorities cannot carry out the death penalty; quite the reverse, with phrase like bearing the sword in vain and he who lives by the sword, dies by the sword.

But we must not forget that the punishment for sin, any sin is death. For the wages of sin is death. Death came into the world by sin. In the Old Testament the blood of innocent animals covered sins. In the New Testament blood of Jesus cleanses us of sin, by his atoning work on the cross. Thank you Jesus!

On a side note there is no mention or principle of prison in the Bible. Jail is a temporary holding place before trial. Most of the New Testament was written from jail! The Old Testament prescribes only three punishments: a fine, a beating or death. Nobody is to be locked up long term with the victim and the rest of society having to pay to keep the guilty incarcerated.

In short, the Bible does not prohibit in principle the death penalty for certain crimes – the state or authorities having the right to carry it out – but it commands believers not to carry it out for themselves but to forgive one another.

Anglican Communion/Church of England (CoE)
Historically supported the death penalty (see Article 37 of the 39 Articles) but came out against it in 1988.

Roman Catholicism/Orthodox

Historically both supported the death penalty but both now oppose the death penalty. The Roman Catholic Church is committed to world–wide abolition.

Baptists

Hold various opinions. For example, the Southern Baptist Convention supports the death penalty, whilst Primitive Baptists are against it.

Methodists

Oppose the death penalty.

Dinosaurs

GENESIS 1:1–19

In the beginning God created the heaven and the earth. And the earth was without form, and void; and darkness was upon the face of the deep. And the Spirit of God moved upon the face of the waters. And God said, Let there be light: and there was light. And God saw the light, that it was good: and God divided the light from the darkness. And God called the light Day, and the darkness he called Night. And the evening and the morning were the first day. And God said, Let there be a firmament in the midst of the waters, and let it divide the waters from the waters. And God made the firmament, and divided the waters which were under the firmament from the waters which were above the firmament: and it was so. And God called the firmament Heaven. And the evening and the morning were the second day. And God said, Let the waters under the heaven be gathered together unto one place, and let the dry land appear: and it was so. And God called the dry land Earth; and the gathering together of the waters called he Seas: and God saw that it was good. And

God said, Let the earth bring forth grass, the herb yielding seed, and the fruit tree yielding fruit after his kind, whose seed is in itself, upon the earth: and it was so. And the earth brought forth grass, and herb yielding seed after his kind, and the tree yielding fruit, whose seed was in itself, after his kind: and God saw that it was good. And the evening and the morning were the third day. And God said, Let there be lights in the firmament of the heaven to divide the day from the night; and let them be for signs, and for seasons, and for days, and years: And let them be for lights in the firmament of the heaven to give light upon the earth: and it was so. And God made two great lights; the greater light to rule the day, and the lesser light to rule the night: he made the stars also. And God set them in the firmament of the heaven to give light upon the earth, And to rule over the day and over the night, and to divide the light from the darkness: and God saw that it was good. And the evening and the morning were the fourth day.

GENESIS 1:20–31

And God said, Let the waters bring forth abundantly the moving creature that hath life, and fowl that may fly above the earth in the open firmament of heaven. And God created great whales, and every living creature that moveth, which the waters brought forth abundantly, after their kind, and every winged fowl after his kind: and God saw that it was good. And God blessed them, saying, Be fruitful, and multiply, and fill the waters in the seas, and let fowl multiply in the earth. And the evening and the morning were the fifth day. And God said, Let the earth bring forth the living creature after his kind, cattle, and creeping thing, and beast of the earth after his kind: and it was so. And God made the beast of the earth after his kind, and cattle after their kind, and every thing that creepeth upon the earth after his kind: and God saw that it was good. And God said, Let us make man in our image, after our likeness: and let them have dominion over the fish of the sea, and over the fowl of the air, and over the cattle, and over all the earth, and over every creeping thing that creepeth upon the earth. So God created man in his own image, in the image of God created he him; male and female created he them. And God blessed them, and God said unto them, Be fruitful, and multiply, and replenish the earth, and subdue it: and have dominion over the fish of the sea, and over the fowl of the air, and over every living thing that moveth upon the earth. And God said, Behold, I have given you every herb bearing seed, which is upon the face of all the earth, and every tree, in the which is the fruit of a tree yielding seed; to you it shall be for meat. And to every beast of the earth, and to every fowl of the air, and to every thing that creepeth upon the earth, wherein there is life, I have given every green herb for meat: and it was so. And God saw every thing that he had made, and, behold, it was very good. And the evening and the morning were the sixth day.

GENESIS 3:1–5

Now the serpent was more subtil than any beast of the field which the LORD God had made. And he said unto the woman, Yea, hath God said, Ye shall not eat of every tree of the garden? And the woman said unto the serpent, We may eat of the fruit of the trees of the garden: But of the fruit of the tree which is in the midst of the garden, God hath said, Ye shall not eat of it, neither shall ye touch it, lest ye die. And the serpent said unto the woman, Ye shall not surely die: For God doth know that in the day ye eat thereof, then your eyes shall be opened, and ye shall be as gods, knowing good and evil.

GENESIS 3:14–15

And the LORD God said unto the serpent, Because thou hast done this, thou art cursed above all cattle, and above every beast of the field; upon thy belly shalt thou go, and dust shalt thou eat all the days of thy life: And I will put enmity between thee and the woman, and between thy seed and her seed; it shall bruise thy head, and thou shalt bruise his heel.

GENESIS 3:20
And Adam called his wife's name Eve; because she was the mother of all living.

EXODUS 20:8-11
Remember the sabbath day, to keep it holy. Six days shalt thou labour, and do all thy work: But the seventh day is the sabbath of the LORD thy God: in it thou shalt not do any work, thou, nor thy son, nor thy daughter, thy manservant, nor thy maidservant, nor thy cattle, nor thy stranger that is within thy gates: For in six days the LORD made heaven and earth, the sea, and all that in them is, and rested the seventh day: wherefore the LORD blessed the sabbath day, and hallowed it.

EXODUS 31:12-17

And the LORD spake unto Moses, saying, Speak thou also unto the children of Israel, saying, Verily my sabbaths ye shall keep: for it is a sign between me and you throughout your generations; that ye may know that I am the LORD that doth sanctify you. Ye shall keep the sabbath therefore; for it is holy unto you: every one that defileth it shall surely be put to death: for whosoever doeth any work therein, that soul shall be cut off from among his people. Six days may work be done; but in the seventh is the sabbath of rest, holy to the LORD: whosoever doeth any work in the sabbath day, he shall surely be put to death. Wherefore the children of Israel shall keep the sabbath, to observe the sabbath throughout their generations, for a perpetual covenant. It is a sign between me and the children of Israel for ever: for in six days the LORD made heaven and earth, and on the seventh day he rested, and was refreshed.

NUMBERS 23:19

God is not a man, that he should lie; neither the son of man, that he should repent: hath he said, and shall he not do it? or hath he spoken, and shall he not make it good?

JOB 40:15–24

Behold now behemoth, which I made with thee; he eateth grass as an ox. Lo now, his strength is in his loins, and his force is in the navel of his belly. He moveth his tail like a cedar: the sinews of his stones are wrapped together. His bones are as strong pieces of brass; his bones are like bars of iron. He is the chief of the ways of God: he that made him can make his sword to approach unto him. Surely the mountains bring him forth food, where all the beasts of the field play. He lieth under the shady trees, in the covert of the reed, and fens. The shady trees cover him with their shadow; the willows of the brook compass him about. Behold, he drinketh up a river, and hasteth not: he trusteth that he can draw up Jordan into his mouth. He taketh it with his eyes: his nose pierceth through snares.

JOB 41

Canst thou draw out leviathan with an hook? or his tongue with a cord which thou lettest down? Canst thou put an hook into his nose? or bore his jaw through with a thorn? Will he make many supplications unto thee? will he speak soft words unto thee? Will he make a covenant with thee? wilt thou take him for a servant for ever? Wilt thou play with him as with a bird? or wilt thou bind him for thy maidens? Shall the companions make a banquet of him? shall they part him among the merchants? Canst thou fill his skin with barbed irons? or his head with fish spears? Lay thine hand upon him, remember the battle, do no more. Behold, the hope of him is in vain: shall not one be cast down even at the sight of him? None is so fierce that dare stir him up: who then is able to stand before me? Who hath prevented me, that I should repay him? whatsoever is under the whole heaven is mine. I will not conceal his parts, nor his power, nor his comely proportion. Who can discover the face of his garment? or who can come to him with his double bridle? Who can open the doors of his face? his teeth are terrible round about. His scales are his pride, shut up together as with a close seal. One is so near to another, that no air can come between them. They are joined one to another, they stick together, that they cannot be sundered. By his neesings a light doth shine, and his eyes are like the eyelids of the morning. Out of his mouth go burning lamps, and sparks of fire leap out. Out of his nostrils goeth smoke, as out of a seething pot or caldron. His breath kindleth coals, and a flame goeth out of his mouth. In his neck remaineth strength, and sorrow is turned into joy before him. The flakes of his flesh are joined together: they are firm in themselves; they cannot be moved. His heart is as firm as a stone; yea, as hard as a piece of the nether millstone. When he raiseth up himself, the mighty are afraid: by reason of breakings they purify themselves. The sword of him that layeth at him cannot hold: the spear, the dart, nor the habergeon. He esteemeth iron as straw, and brass as rotten wood. The arrow cannot make him flee: slingstones are turned with him into stubble. Darts are counted as stubble: he laugheth at the shaking of a spear. Sharp stones are under him: he spreadeth sharp pointed things upon the mire. He maketh the deep to boil like a pot: he maketh the sea like a pot of ointment. He maketh a path to shine after him; one would think the deep to be hoary. Upon earth there is not his like, who is made without fear. He beholdeth all high things: he is a king over all the children of pride.

PSALM 12:6-7

The words of the LORD are pure words: as silver tried in a furnace of earth, purified seven times. Thou shalt keep them, O LORD, thou shalt preserve them from this generation for ever.

PSALM 148:7-8

Praise the LORD from the earth, ye dragons, and all deeps: Fire and hail: snow, and vapour; stormy wind fulfilling his word:

ISAIAH 14:28-30

In the year that king Ahaz died was this burden. Rejoice not thou, whole Palestina, because the rod of him that smote thee is broken: for out of the serpent's root shall come forth a cockatrice, and his fruit shall be a fiery flying serpent. And the firstborn of the poor shall feed, and the needy shall lie down in safety: and I will kill thy root with famine, and he shall slay thy remnant.

ISAIAH 30:6

The burden of the beasts of the south: into the land of trouble and anguish, from whence come the young and old lion, the viper and fiery flying serpent, they will carry their riches upon the shoulders of young asses, and their treasures upon the bunches of camels, to a people that shall not profit them.

ISAIAH 35:7

And the parched ground shall become a pool, and the thirsty land springs of water: in the habitation of dragons, where each lay, shall be grass with reeds and rushes.

ISAIAH 40:6-8
The voice said, Cry. And he said, What shall I cry? All flesh is grass, and all the goodliness thereof is as the flower of the field: The grass withereth, the flower fadeth: because the spirit of the LORD bloweth upon it: surely the people is grass. The grass withereth, the flower fadeth: but the word of our God shall stand for ever.

JEREMIAH 49:33
And Hazor shall be a dwelling for dragons, and a desolation for ever: there shall no man abide there, nor any son of man dwell in it.

JEREMIAH 51:39
And Babylon shall become heaps, a dwellingplace for dragons, an astonishment, and an hissing, without an inhabitant.

MATTHEW 19:3-5

The Pharisees also came unto him, tempting him, and saying unto him, Is it lawful for a man to put away his wife for every cause? And he answered and said unto them, Have ye not read, that he which made them at the beginning made them male and female, And said, For this cause shall a man leave father and mother, and shall cleave to his wife: and they twain shall be one flesh?

JOHN 8:42–47

Jesus said unto them, If God were your Father, ye would love me: for I proceeded forth and came from God; neither came I of myself, but he sent me. Why do ye not understand my speech? even because ye cannot hear my word. Ye are of your father the devil, and the lusts of your father ye will do. He was a murderer from the beginning, and abode not in the truth, because there is no truth in him. When he speaketh a lie, he speaketh of his own: for he is a liar, and the father of it. And because I tell you the truth, ye believe me not. Which of you convinceth me of sin? And if I say the truth, why do ye not believe me? He that is of God heareth God's words: ye therefore hear them not, because ye are not of God.

ROMANS 5:12-14

Wherefore, as by one man sin entered into the world, and death by sin; and so death passed upon all men, for that all have sinned: (For until the law sin was in the world: but sin is not imputed when there is no law. Nevertheless death reigned from Adam to Moses, even over them that had not sinned after the similitude of Adam's transgression, who is the figure of him that was to come.

1 CORINTHIANS 15:20-26

But now is Christ risen from the dead, and become the firstfruits of them that slept. For since by man came death, by man came also the resurrection of the dead. For as in Adam all die, even so in Christ shall all be made alive. But every man in his own order: Christ the firstfruits; afterward they that are Christ's at his coming. Then cometh the end, when he shall have delivered up the kingdom to God, even the Father; when he shall have put down all rule and all authority and power. For he must reign, till he hath put all enemies under his feet. The last enemy that shall be destroyed is death.

EPHESIANS 3:1-12

For this cause I Paul, the prisoner of Jesus Christ for you Gentiles, If ye have heard of the dispensation of the grace of God which is given me to you-ward: How that by revelation he made known unto me the mystery; (as I wrote afore in few words, Whereby, when ye read, ye may understand my knowledge in the mystery of Christ) Which in other ages was not made known unto the sons of men, as it is now revealed unto his holy apostles and prophets by the Spirit; That the Gentiles should be fellow heirs, and of the same body, and partakers of his promise in Christ by the gospel: Whereof I was made a minister, according to the gift of the grace of God given unto me by the effectual working of his power. Unto me, who am less than the least of all saints, is this grace given, that I should preach among the Gentiles the unsearchable riches of Christ; And to make all men see what is the fellowship of the mystery, which from the beginning of the world hath been hid in God, who created all things by Jesus Christ: To the intent that now unto the principalities and powers in heavenly places might be known by the church the manifold wisdom of God, According to the eternal purpose which he purposed in Christ Jesus our Lord: In whom we have boldness and access with confidence by the faith of him.

TITUS 1:2

In hope of eternal life, which God, that cannot lie, promised before the world began;

HEBREWS 1:10

And, Thou, Lord, in the beginning hast laid the foundation of the earth; and the heavens are the works of thine hands:

Are dinosaurs mentioned in the Bible?

Are they the dragons of ancient myth?

What happened to them?

"Dinosaurs are not in the Bible!"

The word dinosaur was only coined in 1841 and so, of course, it does not appear in the Bible. But the word dragon does. Many times. Is it really far-fetched to think of a dragon as a fire-breathing dinosaur? Just look at the description of Leviathan in the book of Job! His breath kindles coals. His neesings (blowing through his nose – they had to invent a word for this because none existed) cause flashes of light. I hope that sparks your interest in this topic but, before we have a close look at the latter part of the book of Job, let us first start at the beginning, with the creation account in Genesis.

Genesis 1 tells us that "In six days the Lord made heaven and the earth and ALL that in them is."

This use of the word 'ALL' means that dinosaurs too were created during these 6 days. On day 5 the marine creatures were made and on day 6, the land creatures.

Exodus 20 and 31 repeat and thereby confirm the statement from Genesis that God created everything in six days. But is it six literal days? Yes, as confirmed by the phrase: "and the evening and the morning the Nth day." This clarifies the meaning of the Hebrew word יוֹם "yom", narrowing its meaning to a literal, 24-hour day.

From a literary standpoint, if you asked a Hebrew writer to indicate a literal, 24-hour day, there is no clearer way that he could do it, but to use evening and morning and numbers. If he meant to indicate a long period of time, or indefinite period of time, there are far better ways he could do it.

We also read that the sun was made on day 4, whereas the plants and vegetation were made on day 3. If, say, the creation days were thousands of years each, wouldn't that be hard on the plant life, having to wait thousands of years for the sun to come up? This is yet more evidence that the days of creation must be literal 24 hour days.

On the strength of the text, as well as logic, one is left with only two choices: either accept the notion of six literal days or disregard the meaning completely. There is no middle ground.

Jesus says in Matthew 19 that the beginning of the creation was when God made Adam and Eve (he made them male and female.) Paul says in Romans 5 that death came as a result of Adam's sin, that is to say that nothing died until man sinned. Death was not part of the creation. Indeed, 1 Corinthians 15 tells us that the last enemy to be destroyed will be death.

In Genesis 3 we have the appearance of the serpent. Not a snake. Whilst a snake can be described as a serpent, serpent can refer to animals living in the sea – a sea serpent – or animals that fly – a winged serpent. Indeed, tales of ancient mariners describe sightings of large, sea serpents. These sightings also happen in the modern era, the Loch Ness monsters being the most well known.

Furthermore, since the serpent was cursed to crawl on its belly afterwards, it more than likely walked prior to the fall.

The serpent speaks to the women. The Bible doesn't say whether the devil possesses the serpent – speaking through it – or whether he takes on the appearance of one (which he is able to do). Nonetheless the result is the temptation, the fall of mankind. God then pronounces curses on Adam, Eve and the serpent.

God curses the serpent to forever crawl on its belly. This would not be much of a curse if the serpent was a snake (as we know it), as it would already be crawling on its belly. So perhaps this serpent was a lizard – having legs – or some sort of flying creature with legs and wings? Or perhaps it was a dinosaur? Snakes are part of the reptile family, along with lizards. Basically they are a legless lizard, like a slow worm. Another interesting fact about lizards is that, in nature, they never stop growing. Perhaps dinosaurs were lizards that grew to an enormous size? They could get very large if they lived as long as Adam did (over 900 years).

The Bible appears to use the word dragon as a generic term for a large lizard/snake-like reptile creature or a particular flying serpent, as mentioned in Isaiah 30:6. Isaiah's description of "fiery flying serpent" does match the general image we have of dragons: breathing fire and being able to fly (which means having wings).

The book of Job, in particular chapters 40 and 41, has compelling descriptions of two creatures that have been the source of much debate.

Chapter 40 mentions a creature called Behemoth. It's a land-based creature that eats grass and has powerful body; has a tail that sways like a cedar tree; has strong and heavy bones, and being the largest animal that God made (chief of the ways of God).

It is also able to wade into the river Jordan and be completely unfazed. Is this a description of a real animal or a piece of poetry? Well, God tells Job to behold (look and see):

"Behold now behemoth"

Job could only behold the creature if it was there with Job at the time.

"which I made with thee"

God created it alongside (with) man, (at the same time)

"he moveth his tail like a cedar".

This creature's tail sways like a cedar tree. In other words it has a very large tail.

The largest land creature to have ever existed has to be the brachiosaurus. It was a four-legged dinosaur with a very long neck and very long tail. It's certainly a better fit with the description given in Job than a hippo or an elephant that Biblical footnotes seem to suggest. Neither of these are the biggest creatures ever (the elephant is today) and nor do they have large tails.

Chapter 41 contains another intriguing creature, called Leviathan. It's a creature that appears to spend a lot of time in the water. Certainly the biblical mention of a fish hook suggests that one would draw it out of the water with a fishing rod (if it were possible, which it plainly isn't).

It clearly has no fear of man:

"Will he make many supplications unto thee? Will he speak soft words unto thee?"

Clearly Job can see this creature and knows of it.

God asks Job whether Job could make the creature serve him or be his pet, or whether he could fight it and win. (No, but Job would remember the fight!) God says that if no one is brave enough stand against this creature, then who can stand against God?

This creature is described as having scales, rather fearsome teeth and, intriguingly, when "neesing", produces flashes of light, as well as breathing out flames and sparks! Smoke also comes out of its nostrils. People are terrified of it, as it is impervious to spears and javelins, and has an armoured underbelly.

Leviathan really fits the mythical description of a dragon, far better than the footnote suggestion of a crocodile. The biblical description is for a much larger creature and one that causes people to flee in terror. The mention of armour and scales for me, rules out the possibility of Leviathan being some sort of plesiosaur. I personally lean more towards a stegosaurus.

It's interesting to note that many species of dinosaurs appear to have large cavities in their heads connected to their airways, which seem to have no other discernable function. This is speculation on my part but maybe they were something to do with breathing fire?

Myths of fire-breathing, dragon-like creatures can be found worldwide in all different cultures. Indeed the Chinese have a dragon as one of the twelve signs of the zodiac. This is interesting as the other eleven signs are all living creatures.

So our question is not "What does the Bible say?", rather "Do you believe what the Bible says?".

Do you believe the descriptions given in the book of Job? If we can't trust the book of Job or even Genesis 1:1, how can we trust John 3:16?

On this point, 2 Timothy 3:16 says "ALL scripture is given by inspiration of God, and is profitable for doctrine, for reproof, for correction, for instruction in righteousness."

Furthermore, Jesus said:

"And he answered and said unto them, Have ye not read, that he which made them at the beginning made them male and female."

Was Jesus lying? Did he have no understanding of modern science? People who believe that the earth is millions of years old should be honest about it: they are claiming that the bible is wrong and that Jesus is a liar.

In short, dinosaurs were created during days 5 and 6 of the creation week, alongside man, approximately 6,000 years ago. After Noah's flood they were probably hunted to extinction or else they struggled to survive in the post–flood conditions. There may be a few alive today.

The majority of denominations accept evolution, in particular theistic evolution, with the creation days being symbolic rather than literal.

Pope Francis has fully accepted evolution.

Divorce & Remarriage

GENESIS 2:18-25

And the LORD God said, It is not good that the man should be alone; I will make him an help meet for him. And out of the ground the LORD God formed every beast of the field, and every fowl of the air; and brought them unto Adam to see what he would call them: and whatsoever Adam called every living creature, that was the name thereof. And Adam gave names to all cattle, and to the fowl of the air, and to every beast of the field; but for Adam there was not found an help meet for him. And the LORD God caused a deep sleep to fall upon Adam, and he slept: and he took one of his ribs, and closed up the flesh instead thereof; And the rib, which the LORD God had taken from man, made he a woman, and brought her unto the man. And Adam said, This is now bone of my bones, and flesh of my flesh: she shall be called Woman, because she was taken out of Man. Therefore shall a man leave his father and his mother, and shall cleave unto his wife: and they shall be one flesh. And they were both naked, the man and his wife, and were not ashamed.

If any man take a wife, and go in unto her, and hate her, And give occasions of speech against her, and bring up an evil name upon her, and say, I took this woman, and when I came to her, I found her not a maid: Then shall the father of the damsel, and her mother,

take and bring forth the tokens of the damsel's virginity unto the elders of the city in the gate: And the damsel's father shall say unto the elders, I gave my daughter unto this man to wife, and he hateth her; And, lo, he hath given occasions of speech against her, saying, I found not thy daughter a maid; and yet these are the tokens of my daughter's virginity. And they shall spread the cloth before the elders of the city. And the elders of that city shall take that man and chastise him; And they shall amerce him in an hundred shekels of silver, and give them unto the father of the damsel, because he hath brought up an evil name upon a virgin of Israel: and she shall be his wife; he may not put her away all his days. But if this thing be true, and the tokens of virginity be not found for

the damsel: Then they shall bring out the damsel to the door of her father's house, and the men of her city shall stone her with stones that she die: because she hath wrought folly in Israel, to play the whore in her father's house: so shalt thou put evil away from among you.

DEUTERONOMY 22:25–29

But if the man encounters a betrothed woman in the open country, and he overpowers her and lies with her, only the man who has done this must die. Do nothing to the young woman, because she has committed no sin worthy of death. This case is just like one in which a man attacks his neighbour and murders him. When he found her in the field, the betrothed woman cried out, but there was no one to save her. If a man encounters a virgin who is not pledged in marriage, and he seizes her and lies with her, and they are discovered, then the man who lay with her must pay the young woman's father fifty shekels of silver,   and she must become his wife because he has violated her. He must not divorce her as long as he lives.

DEUTERONOMY 24:1–4

When a man hath taken a wife, and married her, and it come to pass that she find no favour in his eyes, because he hath found some uncleanness in her: then let him write her a bill of divorcement, and give it in her hand, and send her out of his house. And when she is departed out of his house, she may go and be another man's wife. And if the latter husband hate her, and write her a bill of divorcement, and giveth it in her hand, and sendeth her out of his house; or if the latter husband die, which took her to be his wife; Her former husband, which sent her away, may not take her again to be his wife, after that she is defiled; for that is abomination before the LORD: and thou shalt not cause the land to sin, which the LORD thy God giveth thee for an inheritance.

PROVERBS 6:20–35

My son, keep thy father's commandment, and forsake not the law of thy mother: Bind them continually upon thine heart, and tie them about thy neck. When thou goest, it shall lead thee; when thou sleepest, it shall keep thee; and when thou awakest, it shall talk with thee. For the commandment is a lamp; and the law is light; and reproofs of instruction are the way of life: To keep thee from the evil woman, from the flattery of the tongue of a strange woman. Lust not after her beauty in thine heart; neither let her take thee with her eyelids. For by means of a whorish woman a man is brought to a piece of bread: and the adulteress will hunt for the precious life. Can a man take fire in his bosom, and his clothes not be burned? Can one go upon hot coals, and his feet not be burned? So he that goeth in to his neighbour's wife; whosoever toucheth her shall not be innocent. Men do not despise a thief, if he steal to satisfy his soul when he is hungry; But if he be found, he shall restore sevenfold; he shall give all the substance of his house. But whoso committeth adultery with a woman lacketh understanding: he that doeth it destroyeth his own soul. A wound and dishonour shall he get; and his reproach shall not be wiped away. For jealousy is the rage of a man: therefore he will not spare in the day of vengeance. He will not regard any ransom; neither will he rest content, though thou givest many gifts.

PROVERBS 18:22
Whoso findeth a wife findeth a good thing, and obtaineth favour of the LORD.

MALACHI 2:16
For the LORD, the God of Israel, saith that he hateth putting away: for one covereth violence with his garment,

saith the LORD of hosts: therefore take heed to your spirit, that ye deal not treacherously.

MATTHEW 5:21

It hath been said, Whosoever shall put away his wife, let him give her a writing of divorcement: But I say unto you, That whosoever shall put away his wife, saving for the cause of fornication, causeth her to commit adultery: and whosoever shall marry her that is divorced committeth adultery.

MATTHEW 19:1-12

And it came to pass, that when Jesus had finished these sayings, he departed from Galilee, and came into the coasts of Judaea beyond Jordan; And great multitudes followed him; and he healed them there. The Pharisees also came unto him, tempting him, and saying unto him, Is it lawful for a man to put away his wife for every cause? And he answered and said unto them, Have ye not read, that he which made them at the beginning made them male and female, And said, For this cause shall a man leave father and mother, and shall cleave to his wife: and they twain shall be one flesh? Wherefore they are no more twain, but one flesh. What therefore God hath joined together, let not man put asunder. They say unto him, Why did Moses then command to give a writing of divorcement, and to put her away? He saith unto them, Moses because of the hardness of your hearts suffered you to put away your wives: but from the beginning it was not so. And I say unto you, Whosoever shall put away his wife, except it be for fornication, and shall marry another, committeth adultery: and whoso marrieth her which is put away doth commit adultery. His disciples say unto him, If the case of the man be so with his wife, it is not good to marry. But he said unto them, All men cannot receive this saying, save they to whom it is given. For there are some eunuchs, which were so born from their mother's womb: and there are some eunuchs, which were made eunuchs of men: and there be eunuchs, which have made themselves eunuchs for the kingdom of heaven's sake. He that is able to receive it, let him receive it.

MARK 10:1–12

And he arose from thence, and cometh into the coasts of Judaea by the farther side of Jordan: and the people resort unto him again; and, as he was wont, he taught them again.

And the Pharisees came to him, and asked him, Is it lawful for a man to put away his wife? tempting him. And he answered and said unto them, What did Moses command you? And they said, Moses suffered to write a bill of divorcement, and to put her away. And Jesus answered and said unto them, For the hardness of your heart he wrote you this precept. But from the beginning of the creation God made them male and female. For this cause shall a man leave his father and mother, and cleave to his wife; And they twain shall be one flesh: so then they are no more twain, but one flesh. What therefore God hath joined together, let not man put asunder. And in the house his disciples asked him again of the same matter. And he saith unto them, Whosoever shall put away his wife, and marry another, committeth adultery against her. And if a woman shall put away her husband, and be married to another, she committeth adultery.

LUKE 16:18

Whosoever putteth away his wife, and marrieth another, committeth adultery: and whosoever marrieth her that is put away from her husband committeth adultery.

ROMANS 7:1-3

Know ye not, brethren, (for I speak to them that know the law,) how that the law hath dominion over a man as long as he liveth? For the woman which hath an husband is bound by the law to her husband so long as he liveth; but if the husband be dead, she is loosed from the law of her husband. So then if, while her husband liveth, she be married to another man, she shall be called an adulteress: but if her husband be dead, she is free from that law; so that she is no adulteress, though she be married to another man.

1 CORINTHIANS 6:9-11

Know ye not that the unrighteous shall not inherit the kingdom of God? Be not deceived: neither fornicators, nor idolaters, nor adulterers, nor effeminate, nor abusers of themselves with mankind, Nor thieves, nor covetous, nor drunkards, nor revilers, nor extortioners, shall inherit the kingdom of God. And such were some of you: but ye are washed, but ye are sanctified, but ye are justified in the name of the Lord Jesus, and by the Spirit of our God.

1 CORINTHIANS 7:1-15

Now concerning the things whereof ye wrote unto me: It is good for a man not to touch a woman. Nevertheless, to avoid fornication, let every man have his own wife, and let every woman have her own husband. Let the husband render unto the wife due benevolence: and likewise also the wife unto the husband. The wife hath not power of her own body, but the husband: and likewise also the husband hath not power of his own body, but the wife. Defraud ye not one the other, except it be with consent for a time, that ye may give yourselves to fasting and prayer; and come together again, that Satan tempt you not for your incontinency. But I speak this by permission, and not of commandment. For I would that all men were even as I myself. But every man hath his proper gift of God, one after this manner, and another after that. I say therefore to the unmarried and widows, It is good for them if they abide even as I. But if they cannot contain, let them marry: for it is better to marry than to burn. And unto the married I command, yet not I, but the Lord, Let not the wife depart from her husband: But and if she depart, let her remain unmarried, or be reconciled to her husband: and let not the husband put away his wife. But to the rest speak I, not the Lord: If any brother hath a wife that believeth not, and she be pleased to dwell with him, let him not put her away. And the woman which hath an husband that believeth not, and if he be pleased to dwell with her, let her not leave him. For the unbelieving husband is sanctified by the wife, and the unbelieving wife is sanctified by the husband: else were your children unclean; but now are they holy. But if the unbelieving depart, let him depart. A brother or a sister is not under bondage in such cases: but God hath called us to peace.

1 CORINTHIANS 7:39

The wife is bound by the law as long as her husband liveth; but if her husband be dead, she is at liberty to be married to whom she will; only in the Lord.

1 CORINTHIANS 11:3–12

But I would have you know, that the head of every man is Christ; and the head of the woman is the man; and the head of Christ is God. Every man praying or prophesying, having his head covered, dishonoureth his head. But every woman that prayeth or prophesieth with her head uncovered dishonoureth her head: for that is even all one as if she were shaven. For if the woman be not covered, let her also be shorn: but if it be a shame for a woman to be shorn or shaven, let her be covered. For a man indeed ought not to cover his head, forasmuch as he is the image and glory of God: but the woman is the glory of the man. For the man is not of the woman; but the woman of the man. Neither was the man created for the woman; but the woman for the man. For this cause ought the woman to have power on her head because of the angels. Nevertheless neither is the man without the woman, neither the woman without the man, in the Lord. For as the woman is of the man, even so is the man also by the woman; but all things of God.

GALATIANS 5:19-21

Now the works of the flesh are manifest, which are these; Adultery, fornication, uncleanness, lasciviousness, Idolatry, witchcraft, hatred, variance, emulations, wrath, strife, seditions, heresies, Envyings, murders, drunkenness, revellings, and such like: of the which I tell you before, as I have also told you in time past, that they which do such things shall not inherit the kingdom of God.

EPHESIANS 5:22-33

Wives, submit yourselves unto your own husbands, as unto the Lord. For the husband is the head of the wife, even as Christ is the head of the church: and he is the saviour of the body. Therefore as the church is subject unto Christ, so let the wives be to their own husbands in every thing. Husbands, love your wives, even as Christ also loved the church, and gave himself for it; That he might sanctify and cleanse it with the washing of water by the word, That he might present it to himself a glorious church, not having spot, or wrinkle, or any such thing; but that it should be holy and without blemish. So ought men to love their wives as their own bodies. He that loveth his wife loveth himself. For no man ever yet hated his own flesh; but nourisheth and cherisheth it, even as the Lord the church: For we are members of his body, of his flesh, and of his bones. For this cause shall a man leave his father and mother, and shall be joined unto his wife, and they two shall be one flesh. This is a great mystery: but I speak concerning Christ and the church. Nevertheless let every one of you in particular so love his wife even as himself; and the wife see that she reverence her husband.

HEBREWS 13:4

Marriage is honourable in all, and the bed undefiled: but whoremongers and adulterers God will judge.

So what does the Bible say about:

Marriage?

Divorce?

Remarriage?

Are there any exceptions?

This is perhaps the most difficult chapter for me to write as it affects several brothers and sisters known to me personally. It is a very emotive issue, provoking strong reactions and can lead to serious division in the church. So we will need to tread carefully but, at the same time, being faithful to scripture. Let's begin at the beginning, the book of Genesis.

The passage from Genesis 2 clearly tells us that marriage is the union of one man, leaving his parents and joining to one women so they become 'one flesh'. The Apostle Paul expounds this in the passage from 1 Corinthians in which he states:

"The wife hath not power of her own body, but the husband: and likewise also the husband hath not power of his own body, but the wife."

The husband and wife become one. One unit, one partnership, one family, but with differing roles. The man is to work to earn a living to be able to keep his wife, and to love, honour and protect her. The wife's primary role is to bear and nurture the children and to love, honour and obey her husband. Paul writes of this in Ephesians 5 and 1 Corinthians 11.

Marriage then, is intended as a lifelong heterosexual union, (Genesis 2:24 and Mark 10:8), only broken by the death of either spouse (1 Corinthians 7:39). It is a covenant made between God and a man and a women.

So where does divorce fit in to this? The first time Divorce is mentioned is in the latter half of Deuteronomy 22, where

Moses is instructing the children of Israel on the Law before they enter into the promised land. It is mentioned regarding the possible slandering of the bride's virginity if the bridegroom turns against her. If she is proven to be innocent then the bridegroom has to pay a fine of one hundred shekels to his father-in-law, and remain married to her. Otherwise she is stoned to death. So we see the onus placed on the virginity of the bride. Interesting to note that there is no such requirement on the man to be a virgin.

Later verses in Deuteronomy 22 cover the rape of a betrothed woman, where only the rapist is put to death. If a woman not betrothed is raped, the rapist has to pay fifty shekels to the women's father and the rapist has to marry her. This has the dual purpose of deterring rape and also securing the unfortunate women's future by giving her a husband who then has to support her. This was in a time when women who were no longer virgins were likely to remain unmarried. Adding to the deterrent is that fact that the rapist cannot ever divorce her. They must remain married until he dies.

Deuteronomy 24 also permits divorce. If the bride is no longer pleasing to the bridegroom due to some 'uncleanness' found in her then he may divorce her, writing out a bill of divorce and sending her away. This uncleanness is not adultery as adultery already carried the death penalty (see Deuteronomy 22). The only rule her is that the divorced wife cannot return to her first husband if he second husband dies. Jesus refers to this in Matthew 19, saying that Moses permitted divorce due to the hardness of the Israelites' hearts, but in the beginning (the creation) it was not so.

By the time of the New Testament, the Israelites had already compromised on the Old Testament law. There were two positions held by the Jewish Scribes: Shammai, a conservative only permitted divorce on the grounds of adultery. Hillel, on the other hand, permitted divorce for such grounds as burning meals, talking to other men in the street and just no longer liking one's wife. It is into this situation that Jesus came and that's what we will examine next.

Whilst what the OT says about divorce and remarriage is interesting, it is not paramount for Christians as we are not under the Mosiac Law. What matters is what Jesus said, so let's look at what he said.

Jesus's rule from Mark and Luke is simply that remarriage, after divorce, is adultery.

"And in the house his disciples asked him again of the same matter. And he saith unto them, Whosoever shall put away his wife, and marry another, committeth adultery against her. And if a woman shall put away her husband, and be married to another, she committeth adultery."

"Whosoever putteth away his wife, and marrieth another, committeth adultery: and whosoever marrieth her that is put away from her husband committeth adultery."

Whoever divorces their spouse, and marries another commits adultery AND whoever marries a someone who has been divorced commits adultery.

Adultery is the sexual sin of a married person. Therefore you may be divorced in man's sight but in God's eyes you are still married. God doesn't recognize divorce! Furthermore, the scripture here makes no differentiation been the perpetrator of the divorce and the victim. Sometimes both parties to a divorce are to blame. Sometimes one party is completely innocent, but in either case they are both stuck with the consequences.

Now there is an exception that Jesus made to his rule, and it is found in Matthew 5 and Matthew 19.

"That whosoever shall put away his wife, saving for the cause of fornication, causeth her to commit adultery: and whosoever shall marry her that is divorced committeth adultery."

"Whosoever shall put away his wife, except it be for fornication, and shall marry another, committeth adultery: and whoso marrieth her which is put away doth commit adultery."

So the rule is still anyone who divorces and remarries commits adultery and anyone who married a divorced person commits adultery but with the exception:

"...saving for the cause of fornication/except it be for fornication..."

The problem with the exception clause is that the Lord Jesus didn't use the word adultery which, in the original Greek, is *moicheia*. Instead he used the word *porneia* which is where we get our word pornography from. The King James – I believe correctly – translates this word as 'fornication', although there are three understandings to the meaning of the word *porneia* which we will now consider.

The first is that it is a synonym for the word adultery (*moicheia*). This doesn't seem to be correct because *porneia* and *moicheia* appear in the same list of sexual sins in Galatians 5:19-21 or in 1 Corinthians 6:9-10:

"Know ye not that the unrighteous shall not inherit the kingdom of God? Be not deceived: neither fornicators (*porneia*), nor idolaters, nor adulterers (*moicheia*), nor

141

effeminate, nor abusers of themselves with mankind, Nor thieves, nor covetous, nor drunkards, nor revilers, nor extortioners, shall inherit the kingdom of God."

The second is that it is a broad term for all sexual sin, which would include adultery, fornication, pornography, masturbation, sodomy etc.. The problem with this is that it would make divorce a very common occurrence rather than an exception. It is also the passage those seeking a divorce refer to, and the tendency is for the list of acceptable grounds to grow larger and larger as the need requires.

The third is that it means fornication. This is the sexual sin of an unmarried person i.e. someone having premarital sex. This would make sense especially as this would tie into the OT law and the requirement for a bride to be a virgin. This exception is also only found in Matthew, that most scholars agree was primarily written for Jewish believers:

It begins with family tree of Jesus, going all the way back to Abraham. Furthermore, it refers to the kingdom of heaven rather than the kingdom of God. Religious Jews will not even speak his name! Also, it frequently refers to things being fulfilled that were spoken by the prophets, tying it back to the Old Testament.

This exception therefore is specifically referring to fornication during the betrothal period, before the actual marriage ceremony had taken place. We have an example of this in scripture. When Joseph finds out that his intended, Mary is pregnant he plans to divorce her quietly and send her away, only to have a dream from the Lord, telling her that Mary has not been unfaithful but is instead pregnant by the Holy Spirit. When he awakes, he marries her.

The Jewish betrothal period was similar to the western idea of engagement but was taken more seriously by Jewish people as the betrothed couple were seen as married – as they had agreed marry – even though the couple had not been through the ceremony. So for them, calling off the planned marriage was considered a divorce. I don't believe that the exception would apply to Christians, as today we don't believe people are married until after the ceremony. The only possible use of this exception would be for either the bride or the groom to discover on the marriage bed that the other was not a virgin. The problem here would be that they had both entered a marriage covenant and Jesus's rule would then apply.

This idea of marriage until death comes as such a surprise to the disciples in Matthew 19 that they say that it would be better for a man not to marry to which Jesus rejoins:

"All men cannot receive this saying, save they to whom it is given…. He that is able to receive it, let him receive it."

Is there another possible exception? Yes. In this passage from 1 Corinthians 7, Paul states:

"But if the unbelieving depart, let him depart. A brother or a sister is not under bondage in such cases: but God hath called us to peace."

Firstly, what is meant by the unbelieving here? This is clearly referring to a non-Christian rather than a Christian who no longer believes in their marriage vows as some have argued – which is a real twisting of scripture. The New

Testament clearly distinguishes between believers and unbelievers. Secondly, what is meant by being under bondage? Well, having to stay together if the unbeliever really wants to leave. The meaning of the Greek here is quite literally that the brother or sister is not a slave in this case. The unbelieving spouse who wishes to depart may then proceed from separation to divorce. So one spouse would be divorced but not by their own choice. What could they do then? Well in that case, the verse from 1 Corinthians 7:11 would apply:

"But and if she depart, let her remain unmarried, or be reconciled to her husband: and let not the husband put away his wife."

The divorced person has to stay single i.e. to choose celibacy or else be reconciled to their spouse, and their spouse is not to divorce them.

"For there are some eunuchs, which were so born from their mother's womb: and there are some eunuchs, which were made eunuchs of men: and there be eunuchs, which have made themselves eunuchs for the kingdom of heaven's

sake. He that is able to receive it, let him receive it."
Matthew 19:12

What about cases involving physical violence or emotional abuse? I would understand this passage to would allow for separation and divorce in such cases, but both parties would have to remain single or else be reconciled. God understands that, as sinful human beings, our marriages can go wrong and graciously allows married couples to divorce although he hates divorce as Malachi 2:16 tells us.

What matters most to the Christian is what Jesus said, and he clearly said remarriage after divorce is adultery. And people who commit adultery cannot enter the kingdom of God as Paul warns us in 1 Corinthians 6:9–11:

"Know ye not that the unrighteous shall not inherit the kingdom of God? Be not deceived: neither fornicators, nor idolaters, nor adulterers, nor effeminate, nor abusers of themselves with mankind, Nor thieves, nor covetous, nor drunkards, nor revilers, nor extortioners, shall inherit the kingdom of God."

So if a Christian is in adultery i.e. having married a divorcee or who has divorced and remarried someone else they can't go to heaven. Does that mean they lose their salvation? This is something I struggle with here, namely the doctrine of eternal security. But scripture seems really clear here: that unrepented sexual sin will keep you out of heaven.

So to conclude: if Jesus's words are taken seriously, then I would suggest that the majority of remarriages that take place after divorce are adultery and sinful in God's eyes.

In short, there's no remarriage for divorced people whilst either spouse is alive. One must reconcile with their spouse or remain celibate

Anglican Communion/Church of England (CoE)

Since 2002, remarriage after divorce is permitted at the discretion of the vicar. The vicar may offer a blessing following a civil marriage.

Roman Catholicism/Orthodox

Permits remarriage only after the first marriage has officially been annulled. Members who have had civil marriages after divorce are denied communion until their first marriages have been annulled.

Baptists

Hold a variety of positions. Some will remarry for adultery and abandonment. Other do not permit remarriage at all.

Methodists

Remarriage requests are at the discretion of an individual minister.

Female Leadership

GENESIS 2:15-17

And the LORD God took the man, and put him into the garden of Eden to dress it and to keep it. And the LORD God commanded the man, saying, Of every tree of the garden thou mayest freely eat: But of the tree of the knowledge of good and evil, thou shalt not eat of it: for in the day that thou eatest thereof thou shalt surely die.

GENESIS 2:18-25

And the LORD God said, It is not good that the man should be alone; I will make him an help meet for him. And out of the ground the LORD God formed every beast of the field, and every fowl of the air; and brought them unto Adam to see what he would call them: and whatsoever Adam called every living creature, that was the name thereof. And Adam gave names to all cattle, and to the fowl of the air, and to every beast of the field; but for Adam there was not found an help meet for him. And the LORD God caused a deep sleep to fall upon Adam, and he slept: and he took one of his ribs, and closed up the flesh instead thereof; And the rib, which the LORD God had taken from man, made he a woman, and brought her unto the man. And Adam said, This is now bone of my bones, and flesh of my flesh: she shall be called Woman, because she was taken out of Man. Therefore shall a man leave his father and his mother, and shall cleave unto his wife: and they shall be one flesh. And they were both naked, the man and his wife, and were not ashamed.

GENESIS 3

Now the serpent was more subtil than any beast of the field which the LORD God had made. And he said unto the woman, Yea, hath God said, Ye shall not eat of every tree of the garden? And the woman said unto the serpent, We may eat of the fruit of the trees of the garden: But of the fruit of the tree which is in the midst of the garden, God hath said, Ye shall not eat of it, neither shall ye touch it, lest ye die. And the serpent said unto the woman, Ye shall not surely die: For God doth know that in the day ye eat thereof, then your eyes shall be opened, and ye shall be as gods, knowing good and evil. And when the woman saw that the tree was good for food, and that it was pleasant to the eyes, and a tree to be desired to make one wise, she took of the fruit thereof, and did eat, and gave also unto her husband with her; and he did eat. And the eyes of them both were opened, and they knew that they were naked; and they sewed fig leaves together, and made themselves aprons. And they heard the voice of the LORD God walking in the garden in the cool of the day: and Adam and his wife hid themselves from the presence of the LORD God amongst the trees of the garden. And the LORD God called unto Adam, and said unto him, Where art thou? And he said, I heard thy voice in the garden, and I was afraid, because I was naked; and I hid myself. And he said, Who told thee that thou wast naked? Hast thou eaten of the tree, whereof I commanded thee that thou shouldest not eat? And the man said, The woman whom thou gavest to be with me, she gave me of the tree, and I did eat. And the LORD God said unto the woman, What is this that thou hast done? And the woman said, The serpent beguiled me, and I did eat. And the LORD God said unto the serpent, Because thou hast done this, thou art cursed above all cattle, and above every beast of the field; upon thy belly shalt thou go, and dust shalt thou eat all the days of thy life: And I will put enmity between thee and the woman, and between thy seed and her seed; it shall bruise thy head, and thou shalt bruise his heel. Unto the woman he said, I will greatly multiply thy sorrow and thy conception; in sorrow thou shalt bring forth children; and thy desire shall be to thy husband, and he shall rule over thee. And unto Adam he said, Because thou hast hearkened unto the voice of thy wife, and hast eaten of the tree, of which I commanded thee, saying, Thou shalt not eat of it: cursed is the ground for thy sake; in sorrow shalt thou eat of it all the days of thy life; Thorns also and thistles shall it bring forth to thee; and thou shalt eat the herb of the field; In the sweat of thy face shalt thou eat bread, till thou return unto the ground; for out of it wast thou taken: for dust thou art, and unto dust shalt thou return. And Adam called his wife's name Eve; because she was the mother of all living. Unto Adam also and to his wife did the LORD God make coats of skins, and clothed them. And the LORD God said, Behold, the man is become as one of us, to know good and evil: and now, lest he put forth his hand, and take also of the tree of life, and eat, and live for ever: Therefore the LORD God sent him forth from the garden of Eden, to till the ground from whence he was taken. So he drove out the man; and he placed at the east of the garden of Eden Cherubims, and a flaming sword which turned every way, to keep the way of the tree of life.

GENESIS 3:16

Unto the woman he said, I will greatly multiply thy sorrow and thy conception; in sorrow thou shalt bring forth children; and thy desire shall be to thy husband, and he shall rule over thee.

EXODUS 15:20–21

And Miriam the prophetess, the sister of Aaron, took a timbrel in her hand; and all the women went out after her with timbrels and with dances. And Miriam answered them, Sing ye to the LORD, for he hath triumphed gloriously; the horse and his rider hath he thrown into the sea.

NUMBERS 12:1–9

And Miriam and Aaron spake against Moses because of the Ethiopian woman whom he had married: for he had married an Ethiopian woman. And they said, Hath the LORD indeed spoken only by Moses? hath he not spoken also by us? And the LORD heard it. (Now the man Moses was very meek, above all the men which were upon the face of the earth.) And the LORD spake suddenly unto Moses, and unto Aaron, and unto Miriam, Come out ye three unto the tabernacle of the congregation. And they three came out. And the LORD came down in the pillar of the cloud, and stood in the door of the tabernacle, and called Aaron and Miriam: and they both came forth. And he said, Hear now my words: If there be a prophet among you, I the LORD will make myself known unto him in a vision, and will speak unto him in a dream. My servant Moses is not so, who is faithful in all mine house. With him will I speak mouth to mouth, even apparently, and not in dark speeches; and the similitude of the LORD shall he behold: wherefore then were ye not afraid to speak against my servant Moses? And the anger of the LORD was kindled against them; and he departed.

JUDGES 4:4–10

And Deborah, a prophetess, the wife of Lapidoth, she judged Israel at that time. And she dwelt under the palm tree of Deborah between Ramah and Bethel in mount Ephraim: and the children of Israel came up to her for judgment. And she sent and called Barak the son of

Abinoam out of Kedeshnaphtali, and said unto him, Hath not the LORD God of Israel commanded, saying, Go and draw toward mount Tabor, and take with thee ten thousand men of the children of Naphtali and of the children of Zebulun? And I will draw unto thee to the river Kishon Sisera, the captain of Jabin's army, with his chariots and his multitude; and I will deliver him into thine hand. And Barak said unto her, If thou wilt go with me, then I will go: but if thou wilt not go with me, then I will not go. And she said, I will surely go with thee: notwithstanding the journey that thou takest shall not be for thine honour; for the LORD shall sell Sisera into the hand of a woman. And Deborah arose, and went with Barak to Kedesh. And Barak called Zebulun and Naphtali to Kedesh; and he went up with ten thousand men at his feet: and Deborah went up with him.

2 KINGS 22:14-20

So Hilkiah the priest, and Ahikam, and Achbor, and Shaphan, and Asahiah, went unto Huldah the prophetess, the wife of Shallum the son of Tikvah, the son of Harhas, keeper of the wardrobe; (now she dwelt in Jerusalem in the college;) and they communed with her. And she said unto them, Thus saith the LORD God of Israel, Tell the man that sent you to me, Thus saith the LORD, Behold, I will bring evil upon this place, and upon the inhabitants thereof, even all the words of the book which the king of Judah hath read: Because they have forsaken me, and have burned incense unto other gods, that they might provoke me to anger with all the works of their hands; therefore my wrath shall be kindled against this place, and shall not be quenched. But to the king of Judah which sent you to inquire of the LORD, thus shall ye say to him, Thus saith the LORD God of Israel, As touching the words which thou hast heard; Because thine heart was tender, and thou hast humbled thyself before the LORD, when thou heardest what I spake against this place, and against the inhabitants thereof, that they should become a desolation and a curse, and hast rent thy clothes, and wept before me; I also have heard thee, saith the LORD. Behold therefore, I will gather thee unto thy fathers, and thou shalt be gathered into thy grave in peace; and thine eyes shall not see all the evil which I will bring upon this place. And they brought the king word again.

2 CHRONICLES 34:22–28

And Hilkiah, and they that the king had appointed, went to Huldah the prophetess, the wife of Shallum the son of Tikvath, the son of Hasrah, keeper of the wardrobe; (now she dwelt in Jerusalem in the college:) and they spake to her to that effect. And she answered them, Thus saith the LORD God of Israel, Tell ye the man that sent you to me, Thus saith the LORD, Behold, I will bring evil upon this place, and upon the inhabitants thereof, even all the curses that are written in the book which they have read before the king of Judah: Because they have forsaken me, and have burned incense unto other gods, that they might provoke me to anger with all the works of their hands; therefore my wrath shall be poured out upon this place, and shall not be quenched. And as for the king of Judah, who sent you to inquire of the LORD, so shall ye say unto him, Thus saith the LORD God of Israel concerning the words which thou hast heard; Because thine heart was tender, and thou didst humble thyself before God, when thou heardest his words against this place, and against the inhabitants thereof, and humbledst thyself before me, and didst rend thy clothes, and weep before me; I have even heard thee also, saith the LORD. Behold, I will gather thee to thy fathers, and thou shalt be gathered to thy grave in peace, neither shall thine eyes see all the evil that I will bring upon this place, and upon the inhabitants of the same. So they brought the king word again.

JOEL 2:28–32

And it shall come to pass afterward, that I will pour out my spirit upon all flesh; and your sons and your daughters shall prophesy, your old men shall dream dreams, your young men shall see visions: And also upon the servants and upon the handmaids in those days will I pour out my spirit. And I will shew wonders in the heavens and in the earth, blood, and fire, and pillars of smoke. The sun shall be turned into darkness, and the moon into blood, before the great and the terrible day of the LORD come. And it shall come to pass, that whosoever shall call on the name of the LORD shall be delivered: for in mount Zion and in Jerusalem shall be deliverance, as the LORD hath said, and in the remnant whom the LORD shall call.

ISAIAH 3

For, behold, the Lord, the LORD of hosts, doth take away from Jerusalem and from Judah the stay and the staff, the whole stay of bread, and the whole stay of water, The mighty man, and the man of war, the judge, and the prophet, and the prudent, and the ancient, The captain of fifty, and the honourable man, and the counseller, and the cunning artificer, and the eloquent orator. And I will give children to be their princes, and babes shall rule over them. And the people shall be oppressed, every one by another, and every one by his neighbour: the child shall behave himself proudly against the ancient, and the base against the honourable. When a man shall take hold of his brother of the house of his father, saying, Thou hast clothing, be thou our ruler, and let this ruin be under thy hand: In that day shall he swear, saying, I will not be an healer; for in my house is neither bread nor clothing: make me not a ruler of the people. For Jerusalem is ruined, and Judah is fallen: because their tongue and their doings are against the LORD, to provoke the eyes of his glory. The shew of their countenance doth witness against them; and they declare their sin as Sodom, they hide it not. Woe unto their soul! for they have rewarded evil unto themselves. Say ye to the righteous, that it shall be well with him: for they shall eat the fruit of their doings. Woe unto the wicked! it shall be ill with him: for the reward of his hands shall be given him. As for my people, children are their oppressors, and women rule over them. O my people, they which lead thee cause thee to err, and destroy the way of thy paths. The LORD standeth up to plead, and standeth to judge the people. The LORD will enter into judgment with the ancients of his people, and the princes thereof: for ye have eaten up the vineyard; the spoil of the poor is in your houses. What mean ye that ye beat my people to pieces, and grind the faces of the poor? saith the Lord GOD of hosts. Moreover the LORD saith, Because the daughters of Zion are haughty, and walk with stretched forth necks and wanton eyes, walking and mincing as they go, and making a tinkling with their feet: Therefore the Lord will smite with a scab the crown of the head of the daughters of Zion, and the LORD will discover their secret parts. In that day the Lord will take away the bravery of their tinkling ornaments about their feet, and their cauls, and their round tires like the moon, The chains, and the bracelets, and the mufflers, The bonnets, and the ornaments of the legs, and the headbands, and the tablets, and the earrings, The rings, and nose jewels, The changeable suits of apparel, and the mantles, and the wimples, and the crisping pins, The glasses, and the fine linen, and the hoods, and the vails. And it shall come to pass, that instead of sweet smell there shall be stink; and instead of a girdle a rent; and instead of well set hair baldness; and instead of a stomacher a girding of sackcloth; and burning instead of beauty. Thy men shall fall by the sword, and thy mighty in the war. And her gates shall lament and mourn; and she being desolate shall sit upon the ground.

ACTS 2:14–21

But Peter, standing up with the eleven, lifted up his voice, and said unto them, Ye men of Judaea, and all ye that dwell at Jerusalem, be this known unto you, and hearken to my words: For these are not drunken, as ye suppose, seeing it is but the third hour of the day. But this is that which was spoken by the prophet Joel; And it shall come to pass in the last days, saith God, I will pour out of my Spirit upon all flesh: and your sons and your daughters shall prophesy, and your young men shall see visions, and your old men shall dream dreams: And on my servants and on my handmaidens I will pour out in those days of my Spirit; and they shall prophesy: And I will shew wonders in heaven above, and signs in the earth beneath; blood, and fire, and vapour of smoke: The sun shall be turned into darkness, and the moon into blood, before that great and notable day of the Lord come: And it shall come to pass, that whosoever shall call on the name of the Lord shall be saved.

ACTS 6:1–7

And in those days, when the number of the disciples was multiplied, there arose a murmuring of the Grecians against the Hebrews, because their widows were neglected in the daily ministration. Then the twelve called the multitude of the disciples unto them, and said, It is not reason that we should leave the word of God, and serve tables. Wherefore, brethren, look ye out among you seven men of honest report, full of the Holy Ghost and wisdom, whom we may appoint over this business. But we will give ourselves continually to prayer, and to the ministry of the word. And the saying pleased the whole multitude: and they chose Stephen, a man full of faith and of the Holy Ghost, and Philip, and Prochorus, and Nicanor, and Timon, and Parmenas, and Nicolas a proselyte of Antioch: Whom they set before the apostles: and when they had prayed, they laid their hands on them. And the word of God increased; and the number of the disciples multiplied in Jerusalem greatly; and a great company of the priests were obedient to the faith.

ACTS 18:24-28

And a certain Jew named Apollos, born at Alexandria, an eloquent man, and mighty in the scriptures, came to Ephesus. This man was instructed in the way of the Lord; and being fervent in the spirit, he spake and taught diligently the things of the Lord, knowing only the baptism of John. And he began to speak boldly in the synagogue: whom when Aquila and Priscilla had heard, they took him unto them, and expounded unto him the way of God more perfectly. And when he was disposed to pass into Achaia, the brethren wrote, exhorting the disciples to receive him: who, when he was come, helped them much which had believed through grace: For he mightily convinced the Jews, and that publickly, shewing by the scriptures that Jesus was Christ.

ROMANS 16:1-2

I commend unto you Phebe our sister, which is a servant of the church which is at Cenchrea: That ye receive her in the Lord, as becometh saints, and that ye assist her in whatsoever business she hath need of you: for she hath been a succourer of many, and of myself also.

1 TIMOTHY 2:11-15

Let the woman learn in silence with all subjection. But I suffer not a woman to teach, nor to usurp authority over the man, but to be in silence. For Adam was first formed, then Eve. And Adam was not deceived, but the woman being deceived was in the transgression. Notwithstanding she shall be saved in childbearing, if they continue in faith and charity and holiness with sobriety.

1 TIMOTHY 3:1-13

This is a true saying, If a man desire the office of a bishop, he desireth a good work. A bishop then must be blameless, the husband of one wife, vigilant, sober, of good behaviour, given to hospitality, apt to teach; Not given to wine, no striker, not greedy of filthy lucre; but patient, not a brawler, not covetous; One that ruleth well his own house, having his children in subjection with all gravity; (For if a man know not how to rule his own house, how shall he take care of the church of God?) Not a novice, lest being lifted up with pride he fall into the condemnation of the devil. Moreover he must have a good report of them which are without; lest he fall into reproach and the snare of the devil. Likewise must the deacons be grave, not doubletongued, not given to much wine, not greedy of filthy lucre; Holding the mystery of the faith in a pure conscience. And let these also first be proved; then let them use the office of a deacon, being found blameless. Even so must their wives be grave, not slanderers, sober, faithful in all things. Let the deacons be the husbands of one wife, ruling their children and their own houses well. For they that have used the office of a deacon well purchase to themselves a good degree, and great boldness in the faith which is in Christ Jesus.

TITUS 2:1-8

But speak thou the things which become sound doctrine: That the aged men be sober, grave, temperate, sound in faith, in charity, in patience. The aged women likewise, that they be in behaviour as becometh holiness, not false accusers, not given to much wine, teachers of good things; That they may teach the young women to be sober, to love their husbands, to love their children, To be discreet, chaste, keepers at home, good, obedient to their own husbands, that the word of God be not blasphemed. Young men likewise exhort to be sober minded. In all things shewing thyself a pattern of good works: in doctrine shewing uncorruptness, gravity, sincerity, Sound speech, that cannot be condemned; that he that is of the contrary part may be ashamed, having no evil thing to say of you.

1 CORINTHIANS 11:1–16

Be ye followers of me, even as I also am of Christ. Now I praise you, brethren, that ye remember me in all things, and keep the ordinances, as I delivered them to you. But I would have you know, that the head of every man is Christ; and the head of the woman is the man; and the head of Christ is God. Every man praying or prophesying, having his head covered, dishonoureth his head. But every woman that prayeth or prophesieth with her head uncovered dishonoureth her head: for that is even all one as if she were shaven. For if the woman be not covered, let her also be shorn: but if it be a shame for a woman to be shorn or shaven, let her be covered. For a man indeed ought not to cover his head, forasmuch as he is the image and glory of God: but the woman is the glory of the man. For the man is not of the woman; but the woman of the man. Neither was the man created for the woman; but the woman for the man. For this cause ought the woman to have power on her head because of the angels. Nevertheless neither is the man without the woman, neither the woman without the man, in the Lord. For as the woman is of the man, even so is the man also by the woman; but all things of God. Judge in yourselves: is it comely that a woman pray unto God uncovered? Doth not even nature itself teach you, that, if a man have long hair, it is a shame unto him? But if a woman have long hair, it is a glory to her: for her hair is given her for a covering. But if any man seem to be contentious, we have no such custom, neither the churches of God.

1 CORINTHIANS 14:26-40

How is it then, brethren? when ye come together, every one of you hath a psalm, hath a doctrine, hath a tongue, hath a revelation, hath an interpretation. Let all things be done unto edifying. If any man speak in an unknown tongue, let it be by two, or at the most by three, and that by course; and let one interpret. But if there be no interpreter, let him keep silence in the church; and let him speak to himself, and to God. Let the prophets speak two or three, and let the other judge. If any thing be revealed to another that sitteth by, let the first hold his peace. For ye may all prophesy one by one, that all may learn, and all may be comforted. And the spirits of the prophets are subject to the prophets. For God is not the author of confusion, but of peace, as in all churches of the saints. Let your women keep silence in the churches: for it is not permitted unto them to speak; but they are commanded to be under obedience, as also saith the law. And if they will learn any thing, let them ask their husbands at home: for it is a shame for women to speak in the church. What? came the word of God out from you? or came it unto you only? If any man think himself to be a prophet, or spiritual, let him acknowledge that the things that I write unto you are the

commandments of the Lord. But if any man be ignorant, let him be ignorant. Wherefore, brethren, covet to prophesy, and forbid not to speak with tongues. Let all things be done decently and in order.

GALATIANS 3:28

There is neither Jew nor Greek, there is neither bond nor free, there is neither male nor female: for ye are all one in Christ Jesus.

EPHESIANS 5:22–24

Wives, submit yourselves unto your own husbands, as unto the Lord. For the husband is the head of the wife, even as Christ is the head of the church: and he is the saviour of the body. Therefore as the church is subject unto Christ, so let the wives be to their own husbands in every thing.

PHILIPPIANS 1:1

Paul and Timotheus, the servants of Jesus Christ, to all the saints in Christ Jesus which are at Philippi, with the bishops and deacons: Grace be unto you, and peace, from God our Father, and from the Lord Jesus Christ.

COLOSSIANS 3:18–21

Wives, submit yourselves unto your own husbands, as it is fit in the Lord. Husbands, love your wives, and be not bitter against them. Children, obey your parents in all things: for this is well pleasing unto the Lord. Fathers, provoke not your children to anger, lest they be discouraged.

1 PETER 3:1–6

Likewise, ye wives, be in subjection to your own husbands; that, if any obey not the word, they also may without the word be won by the conversation of the wives; While they behold your chaste conversation coupled with fear. Whose adorning let it not be that outward adorning of plaiting the hair, and of wearing of gold, or of putting on of apparel; But let it be the hidden man of the heart, in that which is not corruptible, even the ornament of a meek and quiet spirit, which is in the sight of God of great price. For after this manner in the old time the holy women also, who trusted in God, adorned themselves, being in subjection unto their own husbands: Even as Sara obeyed Abraham, calling him lord: whose daughters ye are, as long as ye do well, and are not afraid with any amazement.

NB. In the New Testament, the terms bishop, elder, overseer and pastor are used synonymously for the same office in the church.

So our question for this chapter is:

What roles can women perform in church assemblies?

So another controversial topic! I find this somewhat surprising given that the Bible is so clear on this topic, and the reasons for the controversy owe more to modern ideas of gender equality and feminism than lack of clarity in scripture.

Starting in the book of Genesis, Eve is made from Adam's rib (Genesis 2.) Not from his foot that he should trample her underfoot nor from his head that she may rule over him but his rib, so that they should stand side by side.

"But for Adam there was not found an help meet for him. And the LORD God caused a deep sleep to fall upon Adam, and he slept: and he took one of his ribs, and closed up the flesh instead thereof; And the rib, which the LORD God had taken from man, made he a woman, and brought her unto the man."

An help meet (sic) is a 17th century expression meaning a helper, suitable for him.

It is interesting to note that the rib is the only bone in the human body that can grow back if removed, providing the periosteum remains.

Women, like men, are created in the image of God, equal in value, dignity and respect.

The perfection of the garden of Eden was not to last, with the serpent tempting Eve to eat the fruit of the tree of the knowledge of good and evil (Genesis 3).

The Bible doesn't tell us whether Adam was standing next to Eve when the serpent spoke to her, in which case he could have stopped her, or was party to the conversation and went along with it, or whether she was alone, acting independently from him. She was not able to recall God's actual command correctly regarding the fruit of the tree of the knowledge. God's only command to Adam was not to eat of the fruit:

"Of every tree of the garden thou mayest freely eat: But of the tree of the knowledge of good and evil, thou shalt not eat of it: for in the day that thou eatest thereof thou shalt surely die."

Yet Eve said:

"We may eat of the fruit of the trees of the garden: But of the fruit of the tree which is in the midst of the garden, God hath said, Ye shall not eat of it, neither shall ye touch it, lest ye die."

God gave no such command to not touch the tree. Did Adam relay the command incorrectly or did Eve recall the command incorrectly? We don't know. We do know that Adam ate the fruit willingly. Perhaps he knew that God would have to have killed Eve for eating the fruit so ate the fruit himself so that whatever God did to Eve he would have to do to him too. But we must not forget that it was Eve who was deceived and sinned and then Adam sinned:

"Adam was not deceived, but the woman being deceived was in the transgression…"

The serpent tempted Eve – whom had not seen God personally creating the animals – who sinned, but Adam took the blame. He was responsible. Part of the curse is that the mutual equality between Adam and Eve was broken, with woman desiring to have dominion man and man ruling over her.

God kills an animal and makes coats for them before sending them out of the garden. This is an early Illustration of the consequences of sin: something has to die to atone for sin. It also shows God's view of modesty being a coat, rather man's view of modesty being an apron covering the genitals.

This is God creating an order between men and women: men being in charge of women. God bought Eve to Adam and Adam names her. Adam has the authority over Eve. Paul confirms this later in 1 Corinthians 11:

"But I would have you know, that the head of every man is Christ; and the head of the woman is the man; and the head of Christ is God."

So already by Genesis 3, there is a vertical equality between the two sexes and God, but a horizontal inequality between the sexes (God's order for mankind).

"Unto the woman he said, I will greatly multiply thy sorrow and thy conception; in sorrow thou shalt bring forth children; and thy desire shall be to thy husband, and he shall rule over thee."

It is interesting to note that pain during child birth is part of the curse. A very unpopular view nowadays! Also note the passage says "...greatly multiply thy sorrow AND thy conception..." Perhaps before the fall a women's monthly cycle only occurred once a year rather than once a month? I'm pretty sure women would prefer that.

Now, three important women who feature in the Old Testament are: Miriam – a prophetess, Huldah – a prophetess and Deborah – a judge. God chose to use these faithful women to serve him in a particular way. When considering the New Testament passages, these women would be the exception to the rule of male headship. Neither of these women lead a church and they dealt with the Israelites in the Old Testament, not with believers of the New Testament. So they aren't a determining factor in our discussion on church leadership.

Before moving into the New Testament. We need to read Isaiah 3. In this passage we learn about the rather parlous state of Israel: Men having become weak-willed through sin and allowing women to take charge of everything (as a consequence of their own sin), resulting in God taking away all the good things he has given them to guide them and keep them as a nation, and allowing women to rule over them. As a result, people are falling into error and the poor are being neglected. Meanwhile the female rulers are flaunting themselves in costly attire. Female leadership here can be seen as sign that a nation is under God's judgement.

The New Testament is a new paradigm: a new covenant and a new structure for the church, different to the Mosaic covenant.

The books of Timothy and Titus give us the roles in church leadership and the requirements for the roles: the offices of elder and deacon. As mentioned earlier, Paul uses the term bishop, elder, overseer and elder interchangeably, for the same role. For the sake of this book I will use the term elder.

In Timothy, Paul gives us the requirement that the "A bishop must be the husband of one wife..."

This clearly excludes women from becoming elders as women cannot be the husband of one wife. I would contend that this passage also disqualifies unmarried men from becoming elders.

A further requirement for being and elder is the ability to teach. In the earlier passage in 1 Timothy 2, Paul states that he does not permit a woman to teach, and that women are to remain silent in church. So once again we see women excluded from this role. Titus permits women to teach other women.

Paul continues to give the qualifications for deacons:

"Let the deacons be the husbands of one wife, ruling their children and their own houses well."

Once again this would mean that deacons have to be married men.

Contention arises in this passage from Timothy, regarding the translation of γυναῖκας "gynakis". It is translated as 'their wives' in the King James version, but some argue that it should be translated as 'the women', being as the Greek language doesn't distinguish between the two. However this would mean that Paul is giving a list of requirements for women and therefore creating an office of female deacon or deaconess. When read this way the passage reads disjointedly, with 'the women' section being awkwardly inserted in between two sets of requirements for men. It would also contradict "deacons be the husbands of one wife". Furthermore why would there be a different list of qualifications for deacons and deaconesses?

So if women cannot be deacons, how then do we resolve this passage and why does Paul give a list of requirements for the wives of deacons and not for the wives of elders?

Paul's letter to the Philippian church indicates a plurality of bishops (elders) working together to govern that church. No women are involved as they are excluded from being elders. The first deacons in Acts 6 shows them waiting on tables whilst the elders dedicated themselves to prayer and ministry. The deacons therefore appear to work alone, on particular tasks given them by the elders. Perhaps the list of requirements for the wives of deacons is accounting for this

– that the wives of deacons may work alongside and assist their husband in their work: the wives acting as helpmeets.

Another contention is the passage from Romans 16, in which Phoebe is sometimes referred to as a deacon or servant in various translations. In the light of 1 Timothy, I would understand Phoebe being a deacon in the general sense that anybody serving within a church is a deacon i.e. the people who make tea and coffee after a church service and the cleaner who mops the floor.

This is quite different to the office of a deacon. The King James makes this differentiation by referring to Phoebe as a 'servant' rather than 'deacon' despite the Greek word being the same. Those arguing that that Phoebe held the office of a deacon would still not be able to use Phoebe as an example of female leadership in church, as 'apt to teach' is a qualification given to pastors not deacons.

Acts 18 speaks of Priscilla and Aquila meeting and then teaching Apollos, teaching him more perfectly about the ways of God. They taught Apollos in THEIR HOUSE, privately and not in the synagogue. The passage ends with

Apollos moving on to Achaia. Priscilla is never described as being an elder, teaching publicly or leading a church.

1 Corinthians 14 is seen as the most controversial passage regarding women's conduct in the church. There are two prominent positions on this passage:

"Let your women keep silence in the churches: for it is not permitted unto them to speak; but they are commanded to be under obedience, as also saith the law. And if they will learn any thing (sic), let them ask their husbands at home: for it is a shame for women to speak in the church."

One position is that it is an absolute i.e. that women are not to speak at all during a church assembly. The other is that it only applies to women having to keep silence in certain situations whereby, not doing so would assume the authority over men. Certainly, in the previous passages, prophesying in front of the church assembly is allowed:

"Let the prophets speak two or three, and let the other judge. If any thing[SIC] be revealed to another that sitteth by, let the first hold his peace. For ye may all prophesy one by one, THAT ALL MAY LEARN, and all may be comforted."

And clearly women are allowed to pray and prophesy, provided they have a head covering (long hair, not short like a man's else they have dishonoured their heads and ought to be shaved bare!)

"Every man praying or prophesying, having his head covered, dishonoureth his head. But every woman that prayeth or prophesieth with her head uncovered dishonoureth her head: for that is even all one as if she were shaven. For if the woman be not covered, let her also be shorn: but if it be a shame for a woman to be shorn or shaven, let her be covered. For a man indeed ought not to cover his head, forasmuch as he is the image and glory of God: but the woman is the glory of the man." 1 Corinthians 11:4–7

So this passage allows for women to prophesy and pray provided they have long hair and men are to have short hair, so an observable gender differentiation.

"For the man is not of the woman; but the woman of the man. Neither was the man created for the woman; but the woman for the man. For this cause ought the woman to have power on her head because of the angels." 1 Corinthians 11:8-10

"because of the angels."

Interesting reference to Genesis 6 and the fallen angels there.

The view that women are to learn in silence during a church service but later learn from their husbands is reinforced by the passage from 1 Timothy 2:

"Let the woman learn in silence with all subjection. But I suffer not a woman to teach, nor to usurp authority over the man, but to be in silence."

One commonly held position is that chapter 11 of 1 Corinthians is referring to small groups of believers away from the main assembly of the church, that of women being allowed to pray and prophesy, and that chapter 14 is referring to the full assembly of the church i.e. a church service when women are to keep silent. I have some sympathy for this position, however I do not see praying or prophesying as usurping authority over a man in the same way singing and openly worshipping are not. So then the keeping silence in church would only be in regard to usurping authority over men, teaching from the Bible or directing the order of the church service. Ultimately, whether one believes the keep silent passage is an absolute or not is up to one's own personal reading of the text and leading by the Holy Spirit.

So the Bible describes two offices/roles in the church:

Elder – responsible for leading, teaching, preaching, discipline and governance.

Deacon – responsible for serving the church, waiting on tables, taking money to widows, anointing the sick, taking the Lord's supper to people's houses.

Furthermore, we learn from Paul's epistles that no one church has authority over another church, as all churches are subject to the Lord Jesus Christ, and that elders and deacons are selected from within a single church, to serve that church. I believe the apostle Paul's authority over the churches he established ended with his death. Any subsequent new church that established itself would be independent.

In the New Testament Jesus's twelve disciples were all men. The Old Testament prophets and judges were predominantly men. Ephesians 5:22 tells us that spiritual authority rests with men – a universal principle that God has established for the church and the family:

"Wives, submit yourselves unto your own husbands, as unto the Lord. For the husband is the head of the wife, even as Christ is the head of the church: and he is the saviour of the body. Therefore as the church is subject unto Christ, so let the wives be to their own husbands in every thing."

How do New Testament church leadership roles apply to the church today? Let's examine the Church of England with regard to what we have read:

Remember that the Church of England has a hierarchy that does not exist scripturally. The Bible does not have the offices of archbishop, archdeacon or canon. The Bible says nothing about church parliaments (General Synod). Furthermore, newly qualified priests serving in their first placement are often referred to as serving a 'deaconate'. Other uses of the word 'deacon' refer to people serving in a church who are in a transition to becoming a priest. Such people are also called ordinands.

This would mean BIBLICALLY:

No female deacons
No female vicars/priests
No female archdeacons
No female canons
No female deans
No female bishops

CHURCH OF ENGLAND:

Allowed women to become deacons in 1987.
Allowed women to become priests in 1994.

Allowed women to become bishops in 2014.

Theoretically a women can now become archbishop.

The Church of England has clearly put itself in opposition to The Bible on this topic, and although this not essential to salvation, the scriptures are abundantly clear. I do acknowledge that not all churches within the Church of England are the same; some have great teaching and remain faithful to scripture and it is such a church that I would seek out.

Depending on one's understanding of the context of 1 Corinthians 11, then women could be allowed to speak in tongues and prophesy. So women having to keep silence in church would only be in regard to situations where to speak would be taking spiritual authority from the men, in the church assembly/during a service, not asking questions during a sermon or other expositional teaching. I would include women leading the church service from the front, because that could be a stumbling block to a believer from outside that particular congregation – seeing a woman up front, leading a service – creating the assumption that that particular church had female leadership.

In conclusion, I certainly believe that God calls women into ministry, but that doesn't mean that he calls them to be pastors or elders in the church – that would be contradicting scripture. Indeed, scripture should be the first port of call for anybody who believes they have a calling to in order to see scripturally what jobs or service they can undertake.

The Bible has no prohibition on women singing or praying during a church service i.e. doing something that would not take the spiritual authority away from a man. Women are also free to evangelize and to teach other women. Women are not more gullible or more easily deceived than men, else why would they be allowed to teach children? It is children who are easily deceived, and teaching them is a great responsibility.

In short, women cannot hold the offices of Elders or Deacons in a church i.e. no female leadership.

Anglican Communion/Church of England (CoE)

Permits woman in all positions leadership. Individual congregations can opt for male clergy and alternative male bishop oversight (flying bishops).

Roman Catholicism/Orthodox

Does not ordain any women.

Baptists

Hold a variety of positions. Some allow female pastors and deacons. Others only allow female deacons. And others still allow no females in leadership.

Methodists

Has female ministers (UK).

Mary

EXODUS 20:4–6

Thou shalt not make unto thee any graven image, or any likeness of anything that is in heaven above, or that is in the earth beneath, or that is in the water under the earth: Thou shalt not bow down thyself to them, nor serve them: for I the LORD thy God am a jealous God, visiting the iniquity of the fathers upon the children unto the third and fourth generation of them that hate me; And shewing mercy unto thousands of them that love me, and keep my commandments.

LEVITICUS 12

And the LORD spake unto Moses, saying, Speak unto the children of Israel, saying, If a woman have conceived seed, and born a man child: then she shall be unclean seven days; according to the days of the separation for her infirmity shall she be unclean. And in the eighth day the flesh of his foreskin shall be circumcised. And she shall then continue in the blood of her purifying three and thirty days; she shall touch no hallowed thing, nor come into the sanctuary, until the days of her purifying be fulfilled. But if she bear a maid child, then she shall be unclean two weeks, as in her separation: and she shall continue in the blood of her purifying threescore and six days. And when the days of her purifying are fulfilled, for a son, or for a daughter, she shall bring a lamb of the first year for a burnt offering, and a young pigeon, or a turtledove, for a sin offering, unto the door of the tabernacle of the congregation, unto the priest: Who shall offer it before the LORD, and make an atonement for her; and she shall be cleansed from the issue of her blood. This is the law for her that hath born a male or a female. And if she be not able to bring a lamb, then she shall bring two turtles, or two young pigeons; the one for the burnt offering, and the other for a sin offering: and the priest shall make an atonement for her, and she shall be clean.

MATTHEW 1:24–25

Then Joseph being raised from sleep did as the angel of the Lord had bidden him, and took unto him his wife: And knew her not till she had brought forth her firstborn son: and he called his name JESUS.

MATTHEW 12:46-50

While he yet talked to the people, behold, his mother and his brethren stood without, desiring to speak with him. Then one said unto him, Behold, thy mother and thy brethren stand without, desiring to speak with thee. But he answered and said unto him that told him, Who is my mother? and who are my brethren? And he stretched forth his hand toward his disciples, and said, Behold my mother and my brethren! For whosoever shall do the will of my Father which is in heaven, the same is my brother, and sister, and mother.

MARK 6:1-3

And he went out from thence, and came into his own country; and his disciples follow him. And when the sabbath day was come, he began to teach in the synagogue: and many hearing him were astonished, saying, From whence hath this man these things? and what wisdom is this which is given unto him, that even such mighty works are wrought by his hands? Is not this the carpenter, the son of Mary, the brother of James, and Joses, and of Juda, and Simon? and are not his sisters here with us? And they were offended at him.

MARK 15:40

There were also women looking on afar off: among whom was Mary Magdalene, and Mary the mother of James the less and of Joses, and Salome;

LUKE 1:39–47

And Mary arose in those days, and went into the hill country with haste, into a city of Juda; And entered into the house of Zacharias, and saluted Elisabeth. And it came to pass, that, when Elisabeth heard the salutation of Mary, the babe leaped in her womb; and Elisabeth was filled with the Holy Ghost: And she spake out with a loud voice, and said, Blessed art thou among women, and blessed is the fruit of thy womb. And whence is this to me, that the mother of my Lord should come to me? For, lo, as soon as the voice of thy salutation sounded in mine ears, the babe leaped in my womb for joy. And blessed is she that believed: for there shall be a performance of those things which were told her from the Lord. And Mary said, My soul doth magnify the Lord, And my spirit hath rejoiced in God my Saviour.

LUKE 2:21–24

And when eight days were accomplished for the circumcising of the child, his name was called JESUS, which was so named of the angel before he was conceived in the womb. And when the days of her purification according to the law of Moses were accomplished, they brought him to Jerusalem, to present him to the Lord; (As it is written in the law of the Lord, Every male that openeth the womb shall be called holy to the Lord;) And to offer a sacrifice according to that which is said in the law of the Lord, A pair of turtledoves, or two young pigeons.

LUKE 8:19-21

Then came to him his mother and his brethren, and could not come at him for the press. And it was told him by certain which said, Thy mother and thy brethren stand without, desiring to see thee. And he answered and said unto them, My mother and my brethren are these which hear the word of God, and do it.

LUKE 11:27-28

And it came to pass, as he spake these things, a certain woman of the company lifted up her voice, and said unto him, Blessed is the womb that bare thee, and the paps which thou hast sucked. But he said, Yea rather, blessed are they that hear the word of God, and keep it.

ROMANS 3:10-12

As it is written, There is none righteous, no, not one: There is none that understandeth, there is none that seeketh after God. They are all gone out of the way, they are together become unprofitable; there is none that doeth good, no, not one.

1 CORINTHIANS 9:1-5

Am I not an apostle? am I not free? have I not seen Jesus Christ our Lord? are not ye my work in the Lord? If I be not an apostle unto others, yet doubtless I am to you: for the seal of mine apostleship are ye in the Lord. Mine answer to them that do examine me is this, Have we not power to eat and to drink? Have we not power to lead about a sister, a wife, as well as other apostles, and as the brethren of the Lord, and Cephas?

GALATIANS 1:18-19

Then after three years I went up to Jerusalem to see Peter, and abode with him fifteen days. But other of the apostles saw I none, save James the Lord's brother.

1 TIMOTHY 2:1-6

I exhort therefore, that, first of all, supplications, prayers, intercessions, and giving of thanks, be made for all men; For kings, and for all that are in authority; that we may lead a quiet and peaceable life in all godliness and honesty. For this is good and acceptable in the sight of God our Saviour; Who will have all men to be saved, and to come unto the knowledge of the truth. For there is one God, and one mediator between God and men, the man Christ Jesus; Who gave himself a ransom for all, to be testified in due time.

So, regarding Mary:

Was she sinless?

Did she remain a virgin?

Is the Roman Catholic Mary the Mary of scripture?

The first question is answered really by the passage from Romans 3:10-12, in which we learn that there are none righteous (sinless), no not one:

"As it is written, There is none righteous, no, not one: There is none that understandeth, there is none that seeketh after God. They are all gone out of the way, they are together become unprofitable; there is none that doeth good, no, not one."

This is talking about all of mankind of course, as only Jesus was perfect in that he perfectly fulfilled the Mosiac Law and thus was justified by it. No-one else has ever been able to justify themselves by the Law in the Old Testament.

Furthermore, we learn from Luke 2:21-24 that Mary followed the Old Testament requirement to bring two pigeons or two turtle doves to the temple for a sacrifice. This is referencing Leviticus 12, which tells us that one bird was for a SIN offering, the other for a burnt offering. This tells us that Mary was following the Old Testament law and that she was a sinner, as why else would she need to make a sin offering? Mary herself professes her need for a saviour – that she was a sinner – in Luke 1:47, in which she states: "my spirit hath rejoiced in God my Saviour."

It is clear that God clearly blessed and favoured Mary among all women in that she was chosen to bear the Lord Jesus. But that fact that she did and that she had faith didn't miraculously make her sinless, or special to the point where she, as a person, needs to be elevated above all other people as some denominations teach.

Jesus himself refutes this idea of elevating Mary in Luke 11:28, saying: "But he said, Yea rather, blessed are they that hear the word of God, and keep it."

Jesus had brothers and sisters. Matthew 1:24-25 tells that Joseph had normal, marital relations with Mary after she had given birth to Jesus.

Furthermore, Mark 6:1-3 gives us the names of his four (half) brothers: James, Joses, Juda (Jude) and Simon. Later in Mark 15:40 we learn that one of Jesus's sisters is called Salome.

Matthew 12:44-50 confirms that Jesus had siblings, as his mother (Mary) and his brothers came to a house desiring to speak with him but when he heard this, he declared the crowd around him to be his mother, brothers and sisters (his family, in a spiritual way – those who do the will of the Father.)

These verses alone show that Mary cannot possibly be a perpetual virgin as some denominations teach. If she were, then surely Joseph deserves the prize! It would have been extraordinarily usual in first century Israel for a married couple to have remained celibate. And where did all their other children come from?

From this brief study we can safely conclude that the Mary of the Bible is not the Mary of the Roman Catholic church. They are fundamentally different.

The second commandment forbids making graven images (statutes) or idols. Roman Catholic churches are full of them. And they go further in that they venerate (worship) statues, bowing down before them and praying to them. This is idolatry, breaking of the first commandment.

Mary cannot hear our prayers in heaven. Only God can do that. She cannot mediate between mankind and God. Only Jesus can do that, as 1 Timothy 2:5 states:

"For there is one God, and one mediator between God and men, the man Christ Jesus; Who gave himself a ransom for all, to be testified in due time."

Roman Catholics need to read their bibles and to realize that they are being taught falsehood. They need to repent and place their faith in the Lord Jesus Christ, and not Mary.

Please be assured that I do not hate Roman Catholics. I love them and want them to be saved, but the truth by which they can be saved can only be found in scripture.

In short, Mary was a sinner, just like the rest of us but God chose to use her to bring forth the Saviour.

Slavery

Come, and let us sell him to the Ishmeelites, and let not our hand be upon him; for he is our brother and our flesh. And his brethren were content. Then there passed by Midianites merchantmen; and they drew and lifted up Joseph out of the pit, and sold Joseph to the Ishmeelites for twenty pieces of silver: and they brought Joseph into Egypt.

GENESIS 29:14–30

And Laban said to him, Surely thou art my bone and my flesh. And he abode with him the space of a month. And Laban said unto Jacob, Because thou art my brother, shouldest thou therefore serve me for nought? tell me, what shall thy wages be? And Laban had two daughters: the name of the elder was Leah, and the name of the younger was Rachel. Leah was tender eyed; but Rachel was beautiful and well favoured. And Jacob loved Rachel; and said, I will serve thee seven years for Rachel thy younger daughter. And Laban said, It is better that I give her to thee, than that I should give her to another man: abide with me. And Jacob served seven years for Rachel; and they seemed unto him but a few days, for the love he had to her. And Jacob said unto Laban, Give me my wife, for my days are fulfilled, that I may go in unto her. And Laban gathered together all the men of the place, and made a feast. And it came to pass in the evening, that he took Leah his daughter, and brought her to him; and he went in unto her. And Laban gave unto his daughter Leah Zilpah his maid for an handmaid. And it came to pass, that in the morning, behold, it was Leah: and he said to Laban, What is this thou hast done unto me? did not I serve with thee for Rachel? wherefore then hast thou beguiled me? And Laban said, It must not be so done in our country, to give the younger before the firstborn. Fulfil her week, and we will give thee this also for the service which thou shalt serve with me yet seven other years. And Jacob did so, and fulfilled her week: and he gave him Rachel his daughter to wife also. And Laban gave to Rachel his daughter Bilhah his handmaid to be her maid. And he went in also unto Rachel, and he loved also Rachel more than Leah, and served with him yet seven other years.

EXODUS 21:1-11

Now these are the judgments which thou shalt set before them. If thou buy an Hebrew servant, six years he shall serve: and in the seventh he shall go out free for nothing. If he came in by himself, he shall go out by himself: if he were married, then his wife shall go out with him. If his master have given him a wife, and she have born him sons or daughters; the

wife and her children shall be her master's, and he shall go out by himself. And if the servant shall plainly say, I love my master, my wife, and my children; I will not go out free: Then his master shall bring him unto the judges; he shall also bring him to the door, or unto the door post; and his master shall bore his ear through with an aul; and he shall serve him for ever. And if a man sell his daughter to be a maidservant, she shall not go out as the menservants do. If she please not her master, who hath betrothed her to himself, then shall he let her be redeemed: to sell her unto a strange nation he shall have no power, seeing he hath dealt deceitfully with her. And if he have betrothed her unto his son, he shall deal with her after the manner of daughters. If he take him another wife; her food, her raiment, and her duty of marriage, shall he not diminish. And if he do not these three unto her, then shall she go out free without money.

EXODUS 21:16

And he that stealeth a man, and selleth him, or if he be found in his hand, he shall surely be put to death.

EXODUS 21:20–21

And if a man smite his servant, or his maid, with a rod, and he die under his hand; he shall be surely punished. Notwithstanding, if he continue a day or two, he shall not be punished: for he is his money.

EXODUS 21:26–27

And if a man smite the eye of his servant, or the eye of his maid, that it perish; he shall let him go free for his eye's sake. And if he smite out his manservant's tooth, or his maidservant's tooth; he shall let him go free for his tooth's sake.

LEVITICUS 25:39–46

And if thy brother that dwelleth by thee be waxen poor, and be sold unto thee; thou shalt not compel him to serve as a bondservant: But as an hired servant, and as a sojourner, he shall be with thee, and shall serve thee unto the year of jubile: And then shall he depart from thee, both he and his children with him, and shall return unto his own family, and unto the possession of his fathers shall he return. For they are my servants, which I brought forth out of the land of Egypt: they shall not be sold as bondmen. Thou shalt not rule over him with rigour; but shalt fear thy God. Both thy bondmen, and thy bondmaids, which thou shalt have, shall be of the heathen that are round about you; of them shall ye buy bondmen and bondmaids. Moreover of the children of the strangers that do sojourn among you, of them shall ye buy, and of their families that are with you, which they begat in your land: and they shall be your possession. And ye shall take them as an inheritance for your children after you, to inherit them for a possession; they shall be your bondmen for ever: but over your brethren the children of Israel, ye shall not rule one over another with rigour.

DEUTERONOMY 15:12–18

And if thy brother, an Hebrew man, or an Hebrew woman, be sold unto thee, and serve thee six years; then in the seventh year thou shalt let him go free from thee. And when thou sendest him out free from thee, thou shalt not let him go away empty: Thou shalt furnish him liberally out of thy flock, and out of thy floor, and out of thy winepress:

of that wherewith the LORD thy God hath blessed thee thou shalt give unto him. And thou shalt remember that thou wast a bondman in the land of Egypt, and the LORD thy God redeemed thee: therefore I command thee this thing to day. And it shall be, if he say unto thee, I will not go away from thee; because he loveth thee and thine house, because he is well with thee; Then thou shalt take an aul, and thrust it through his ear unto the door, and he shall be thy servant for ever. And also unto thy maidservant thou shalt do likewise.

It shall not seem hard unto thee, when thou sendest him away free from thee; for he hath been worth a double hired servant to thee, in serving thee six years: and the LORD thy God shall bless thee in all that thou doest.

DEUTERONOMY 24:7

If a man be found stealing any of his brethren of the children of Israel, and maketh merchandise of him, or selleth him; then that thief shall die; and thou shalt put evil away from among you.

JOSHUA 9:22-44

And Joshua called for them, and he spake unto them, saying, Wherefore have ye beguiled us, saying, We are very far from you; when ye dwell among us? Now therefore ye are cursed, and there shall none of you be freed from being bondmen, and hewers of wood and drawers of water for the house of my God.

1 CHRONICLES 2:34–36
Now Sheshan had no sons, only daughters, but Sheshan had an Egyptian slave whose name was Jarha. So Sheshan gave his daughter in marriage to Jarha his slave, and she bore him Attai. Attai fathered Nathan, and Nathan fathered Zabad.

1 TIMOTHY 1:8–11
But we know that the law is good, if a man use it lawfully; Knowing this, that the law is not made for a righteous man, but for the lawless and disobedient, for the ungodly and for sinners, for unholy and profane, for murderers of fathers and murderers of mothers, for manslayers, For whoremongers, for them that defile themselves with mankind, for menstealers, for liars, for perjured persons, and if there be any other thing that is contrary to sound

doctrine; According to the glorious gospel of the blessed God, which was committed to my trust.

TITUS 2:9-10

Exhort servants to be obedient unto their own masters, and to please them well in all things; not answering again; Not purloining, but shewing all good fidelity; that they may adorn the doctrine of God our Saviour in all things.

PHILEMON

Paul, a prisoner of Jesus Christ, and Timothy our brother, unto Philemon our dearly beloved, and fellowlabourer, And to our beloved Apphia, and Archippus our fellowsoldier, and to the church in thy house: Grace to you, and peace, from God our Father and the Lord Jesus Christ. I thank my God, making mention of thee always in my prayers, Hearing of thy love and faith, which thou hast toward the Lord Jesus, and toward all saints; That the communication of thy faith may become effectual by the acknowledging of every good thing which is in you in Christ Jesus. For we have great joy and consolation in thy love, because the bowels of the saints are refreshed by thee, brother. Wherefore, though I might be much bold in

Christ to enjoin thee that which is convenient, Yet for love's sake I rather beseech thee, being such an one as Paul the aged, and now also a prisoner of Jesus Christ. I beseech thee for my son Onesimus, whom I have begotten in my bonds: Which in time past was to thee unprofitable, but now profitable to thee and to me: Whom I have sent again: thou therefore receive him, that is, mine own bowels: Whom I would have retained with me, that in thy stead he might have ministered unto me in the bonds of the gospel: But without thy mind would I do nothing; that thy benefit should not be as it were of necessity, but willingly. For perhaps he therefore departed for a season, that thou shouldest receive him for ever; Not now as a servant, but above a servant, a brother beloved, specially to me, but how much more unto thee, both in the flesh, and in the Lord? If thou count me therefore a partner, receive him as myself. If he hath wronged thee, or oweth thee ought, put that on mine account; I Paul have written it with mine own hand, I will repay it: albeit I do not say to thee how thou owest unto me even thine own self besides. Yea, brother, let me have joy of thee in the Lord: refresh my bowels in the Lord. Having confidence in thy obedience I wrote unto thee, knowing that thou wilt also do more than I say. But withal prepare me also a lodging: for I trust that through your prayers I shall be given unto you. There salute thee Epaphras, my fellowprisoner in Christ Jesus; Marcus, Aristarchus, Demas, Lucas, my fellowlabourers. The grace of our Lord Jesus Christ be with your spirit. Amen. {Written from Rome to Philemon, by Onesimus a servant.}

1 CORINTHIANS 12:13

For by one Spirit are we all baptized into one body, whether we be Jews or Gentiles, whether we be bond or free; and have been all made to drink into one Spirit.

GALATIANS 3:26-29

For ye are all the children of God by faith in Christ Jesus. For as many of you as have been baptized into Christ have put on Christ. There is neither Jew nor Greek, there is neither bond nor free, there is neither male nor female: for ye are all one in Christ Jesus. And if ye be Christ's, then are ye Abraham's seed, and heirs according to the promise.

COLOSSIANS 3:22-25

Servants, obey in all things your masters according to the flesh; not with eyeservice, as menpleasers; but in singleness of heart, fearing God: And whatsoever ye do, do it heartily, as to the Lord, and not unto men; Knowing that of the Lord ye shall receive the reward of the inheritance: for ye serve the Lord Christ. But he that doeth wrong shall receive for the wrong which he hath done: and there is no respect of persons.

COLOSSIANS 4:1

Masters, give unto your servants that which is just and equal; knowing that ye also have a Master in heaven.

EPHESIANS 6:5–9

Servants, be obedient to them that are your masters according to the flesh, with fear and trembling, in singleness of your heart, as unto Christ; Not with eyeservice, as menpleasers; but as the servants of Christ, doing the will of God from the heart; With good will doing service, as to the Lord, and not to men: Knowing that whatsoever good thing any man doeth, the same shall he receive of the Lord, whether he be bond or free.

And, ye masters, do the same things unto them, forbearing threatening: knowing that your Master also is in heaven; neither is there respect of persons with him.

1 PETER 2:18–20

Servants, be subject to your masters with all fear; not only to the good and gentle, but also to the froward. For this is thankworthy, if a man for conscience toward God endure grief, suffering wrongfully. For what glory is it, if, when ye be buffeted for your faults, ye shall take it patiently? but if, when ye do well, and suffer for it, ye take it patiently, this is acceptable with God.

Does the Bible permit slavery?

Are there different types of slavery?

Is all slavery immoral?

The first thing to say on this topic is that slavery has existed for a long time, long before Moses received the OT law from God on Mount Sinai. The second thing to say is that there is more than one form of slavery in the world.

Slaves in the ancient world who ran away from their owners/ masters could be executed or returned to their masters for a beating. Rape and beatings were commonplace for slaves. They had no personal possessions of their own; they were considered to be possessions. Slavery in the Roman Empire is well documented.

The Bible mentions two types of slavery, neither of them being chattel slavery i.e. involving the kidnapping of a person and their sale to another, because kidnapping carried the death penalty, either for the kidnapper or for the person found in possession of the kidnapped. (Exodus 21 & Deuteronomy 24).

In the Bible, the term bondservant and slave are effectively synonyms.

Exodus 21 gives the laws regulating slavery, specifically Hebrew slaves. We need to understand that the slavery described here was more a form of indentured servitude, lasting a maximum of 6 years after which the servant would go free. No one could be forced to become a slave. (Leviticus 25:39).

If the slave entered servitude with his wife, he would go out with his wife. If his master gave him a wife and they had children, the wife and children would belong to the master. So he would have to go out without her or he could become a bondservant (slave) for life. (Exodus 21).

Later verses control the treatment of slaves, particularly Exodus 21:20-21:

"And if a man smite his servant, or his maid, with a rod, and he die under his hand; he shall be surely punished. Notwithstanding, if he continue a day or two, he shall not be punished: for he is his money."

If a man struck his servant (slave) and killed them, he would be punished; eye for an eye, a tooth for a tooth. (Executed under the OT law in Exodus 21).

And and continuing in Exodus 21:26-27:

"And if a man smite the eye of his servant, or the eye of his maid, that it perish; he shall let him go free for his eye's sake. And if he smite out his manservant's tooth, or his maidservant's tooth; he shall let him go free for his tooth's sake."

Any physical injury caused to the slave would lead to their freedom.

Leviticus 25 allowed poor people to sell themselves voluntarily into servitude, again for a maximum of six years. Their masters were not to treat them harshly but in fear of God.

Deuteronomy 15 tells masters not to send their bondservants away empty handed but with good share from their own storehouses.

When Joshua led the conquest of the promised land, God instructed him to drive the inhabitants out or otherwise kill them in battle. In Joshua 9, the Gibeonites were able to trick the Israelites into agreeing to a treaty, allowing them to stay in the land and not be killed. When Joshua discovered their deception, he cursed them and told them they would never be freed from servitude, which they accepted (voluntarily).

So at the close of the first five books of the OT, we see two types of slavery. Both are voluntary. The Hebrews serving for a maximum of six years unless they agree to extend servitude for life, and the Gentiles never being freed. We also read that Gentiles could buy Hebrew slaves whom could be redeemed. We also read that slaves had to be treated well in the fear of God.

In 1 CHRONICLES 2:34-36, we learn that slaves could inherit. This is very different to chattel slavery where the slaves have no possessions. Indeed they are possessions. It would have been unheard of for a plantation owner to allow one of his slaves to marry into the family and inherit!

In Genesis 29, after Jacob has fled Esau and gone to his Uncle Laban, Jacob is promised Rachael if he works for Laban seven years – a period of indentured servitude – but he is tricked into marrying Leah. He then has to work a further seven years before he can finally marry Rachael.

In summary, the OT gives laws regulating slavery in the form of indentured servitude, whereas the NT gives advice to those in slavery at the time of the Roman occupation and empire. It does not endorse it. The OT laws are no longer applicable since the end of the theocratic state of Israel.

In the book of Philemon, the apostle Paul has clearly met a runaway slave called Onesimus. Onesimus has become a believer and Paul asks Philemon to accept Onesimus back as a brother, not a servant – effectively asking for his freedom – just as he would accept Paul. Paul offers to pay any debts Onesimus owed. Ultimately in Christ we are all equal, brothers and sisters. (Galatians 3:26-29)

Antebellum slavery allowed people — considered legal property — to be bought, sold and owned forever, and was lawful and supported by the United States and European powers from the 16th – 18th centuries. It was fuelled by racism, which regarded non white people as little more than animals. It would have been illegal and punishable by death if its proponents had been held to the OT law. It was Christians and their understanding of scripture that led to its abolition.

In short, the Bible does acknowledges the existence of slavery, and introduced laws governing it. The Biblical form of slavery was consensual and often a last resort for the destitute, and would generally last a period six years with a few exceptions.

All denominations today would condemn slavery, if it were still legal here in the UK. Indentured servitude was a feature of Old Testament Israel.

The Sabbath

GENESIS 2:1–3

Thus the heavens and the earth were finished, and all the host of them. And on the seventh day God ended his work which he had made; and he rested on the seventh day from all his work which he had made. And God blessed the seventh day, and sanctified it: because that in it he had rested from all his work which God created and made.

EXODUS 16:22–30

And it came to pass, that on the sixth day they gathered twice as much bread, two omers for one man: and all the rulers of the congregation came and told Moses. And he said unto them, This is that which the LORD hath said, To morrow is the rest of the holy sabbath unto the LORD: bake that which ye will bake to day, and seethe that ye will seethe; and that which remaineth over lay up for you to be kept until the morning. And they laid it up till the morning, as Moses bade: and it did not stink, neither was there any worm therein. And Moses said, Eat that to day; for to day is a sabbath unto the LORD: to day ye shall not find it in the field. Six days ye shall gather it; but on the seventh day, which is the sabbath, in it there shall be none. And it came to pass, that there went out some of the people on the seventh day for to gather, and they found none. And the LORD said unto Moses, How long refuse ye to keep my commandments and my laws? See, for that the LORD hath given you the sabbath, therefore he giveth you on the sixth day the bread of two days; abide ye every man in his place, let no man go out of his place on the seventh day. So the people rested on the seventh day.

EXODUS 20:1–17

And God spake all these words, saying, I am the LORD thy God, which have brought thee out of the land of Egypt, out of the house of bondage. Thou shalt have no other gods before me. Thou shalt not make unto thee any graven image, or any likeness of any thing that is in heaven above, or that is in the earth beneath, or that is in the water under the earth: Thou shalt not bow down thyself to them, nor serve them: for I the LORD thy God am a jealous God, visiting the iniquity of the fathers upon the children unto the third and fourth generation of them that hate me; And shewing mercy unto thousands of them that love me, and keep my commandments. Thou shalt not take the name of the LORD thy God in vain; for the LORD will not hold him guiltless that taketh his name in vain. Remember the sabbath day, to keep it holy. Six days shalt thou labour, and do all thy work: But the seventh day is the sabbath of the LORD thy God: in it thou shalt not do any work, thou, nor thy son, nor thy daughter, thy manservant, nor thy maidservant, nor thy cattle, nor thy stranger that is within thy gates: For in six days the LORD made heaven and earth, the sea, and all that in them is, and rested the seventh day: wherefore the LORD blessed the sabbath day, and hallowed it. Honour thy father and thy mother: that thy days may be long upon the land which the LORD thy God giveth thee. Thou shalt not kill. Thou shalt not commit adultery. Thou shalt not steal. Thou shalt not bear false witness against thy neighbour. Thou shalt not covet thy neighbour's house, thou shalt not covet thy neighbour's wife, nor his manservant, nor his maidservant, nor his ox, nor his ass, nor any thing that is thy neighbour's.

EXODUS 31:12–17

And the LORD spake unto Moses, saying, Speak thou also unto the children of Israel, saying, Verily my sabbaths ye shall keep: for it is a sign between me and you throughout your generations; that ye may know that I am the LORD that doth sanctify you. Ye shall keep the sabbath therefore; for it is holy unto you: every one that defileth it shall surely be put to death: for whosoever doeth any work therein, that soul shall be cut off from among his people. Six days may work be done; but in the seventh is the sabbath of rest, holy to the LORD: whosoever doeth any work in the sabbath day, he shall surely be put to death. Wherefore the children of Israel shall keep the sabbath, to observe the sabbath throughout their generations, for a perpetual covenant. It is a sign between me and the children of Israel for ever: for in six days the LORD made heaven and earth, and on the seventh day he rested, and was refreshed.

EXODUS 35:2–3

Six days shall work be done, but on the seventh day there shall be to you an holy day, a sabbath of rest to the LORD: whosoever doeth work therein shall be put to death. Ye shall kindle no fire throughout your habitations upon the sabbath day.

DEUTERONOMY 5:6–21

I am the LORD thy God, which brought thee out of the land of Egypt, from the house of bondage. Thou shalt have none other gods before me. Thou shalt not make thee any graven image, or any likeness of any thing that is in heaven above, or that is in the earth beneath, or that is in the waters beneath the earth: Thou shalt not bow down thyself unto them, nor serve them: for I the LORD thy God am a jealous God, visiting the iniquity of the fathers upon the children unto the third and fourth generation of them that hate me, And shewing mercy unto thousands of them that love me and keep my commandments. Thou shalt not take the name of the LORD thy God in vain: for the LORD will not hold him guiltless that taketh his name in vain. Keep the sabbath day to sanctify it, as the LORD thy God hath commanded thee. Six days thou shalt labour, and do all thy work: But the seventh day is the sabbath of the LORD thy God: in it thou shalt not do any work, thou, nor thy son, nor thy daughter, nor thy manservant, nor thy maidservant, nor thine ox, nor thine ass, nor any of thy cattle, nor thy stranger that is within thy gates; that thy manservant and thy maidservant may rest as well as thou. And remember that thou wast a servant in the land of Egypt, and that the LORD thy God brought thee out thence through a mighty hand and by a stretched out arm: therefore the LORD thy God commanded thee to keep the sabbath day. Honour thy father and thy mother, as the LORD thy God hath commanded thee; that thy days may be prolonged, and that it may go well with thee, in the land which the LORD thy God giveth thee. Thou shalt not kill. Neither shalt thou commit adultery. Neither shalt thou steal. Neither shalt thou bear false witness against thy neighbour. Neither shalt thou desire thy neighbour's wife, neither shalt thou covet thy neighbour's house, his field, or his manservant, or his maidservant, his ox, or his ass, or any thing that is thy neighbour's.

NEHEMIAH 9:13-14

Thou camest down also upon mount Sinai, and spakest with them from heaven, and gavest them right judgments, and true laws, good statutes and commandments: And madest known unto them thy holy sabbath, and commandedst them precepts, statutes, and laws, by the hand of Moses thy servant:

EZEKIEL 20:1-20

And it came to pass in the seventh year, in the fifth month, the tenth day of the month, that certain of the elders of Israel came to inquire of the LORD, and sat before me. Then came the word of the LORD unto me, saying, Son of man, speak unto the elders of Israel, and say unto them, Thus saith the Lord GOD; Are ye come to inquire of me? As I live, saith the Lord GOD, I will not be inquired of by you. Wilt thou judge them, son of man, wilt thou judge them? cause them to know the abominations of their fathers: And say unto them, Thus saith the Lord GOD; In the day when I chose Israel, and lifted up mine hand unto the seed of the house of Jacob, and made myself known unto them in the land of Egypt, when I lifted up mine hand unto them, saying, I am the LORD your God; In the day that I lifted up mine hand unto them, to bring them forth of the land of Egypt into a land that I had espied for them, flowing with milk and honey, which is the glory of all lands: Then said I unto them, Cast ye away every man the abominations of his eyes, and defile not yourselves with the idols of Egypt: I am the LORD your God. But they rebelled against me, and would not hearken unto me: they did not every man cast away the abominations of their eyes, neither did they forsake the idols of Egypt: then I said, I will pour out my fury upon them, to accomplish my anger against them in the midst of the land of Egypt. But I wrought for my name's sake, that it should not be polluted before the heathen, among whom they were, in whose sight I made myself known unto them, in bringing them forth out of the land of Egypt. Wherefore I caused them to go forth out of the land of Egypt, and brought them into the wilderness. And I gave them my statutes, and shewed them my judgments, which if a man do, he shall even live in them. Moreover also I gave them my sabbaths, to be a sign between me and them, that they might know that I am the LORD that sanctify them. But the house of Israel rebelled against me in the wilderness: they walked not in my statutes, and they despised my judgments, which if a man do, he shall even live in them; and my sabbaths they greatly polluted: then I said, I would pour out my fury upon them in the wilderness, to consume them. But I wrought for my name's sake, that it should not be polluted before the heathen, in whose sight I brought them out. Yet also I lifted up my hand unto them in the wilderness, that I would not bring them into the land which I had given them, flowing with milk and honey, which is the glory of all lands; Because they despised my judgments, and walked not in my statutes, but polluted my sabbaths: for their heart went after their idols. Nevertheless mine eye spared them from destroying them, neither did I make an end of them in the wilderness. But I said unto their children in the wilderness, Walk ye not in the statutes of your fathers, neither observe their judgments, nor defile yourselves with their idols: I am the LORD your God; walk in my statutes, and keep my judgments, and do them; And hallow my sabbaths; and they shall be a sign between me and you, that ye may know that I am the LORD your God.

MATTHEW 12:1-8

At that time Jesus went on the sabbath day through the corn; and his disciples were an hungred, and began to pluck the ears of corn, and to eat. But when the Pharisees saw it, they said unto him, Behold, thy disciples do that which is not lawful to do upon the sabbath day. But he said unto them, Have ye not read what David did, when he was an hungred, and they that were with him; How he entered into the house of God, and did eat the shewbread, which was not lawful for him to eat, neither for them which were with him, but only for the priests? Or have ye not read in the law, how that on the sabbath days the priests in the temple profane the sabbath, and are blameless? But I say unto you, That in this place is one greater than the temple. But if ye had known what this meaneth, I will have mercy, and not sacrifice, ye would not have condemned the guiltless. For the Son of man is Lord even of the sabbath day.

MARK 2:23-28

And it came to pass, that he went through the corn fields on the sabbath day; and his disciples began, as they went, to pluck the ears of corn. And the Pharisees said unto him, Behold, why do they on the sabbath day that which is not lawful? And he said unto them, Have ye never read what David did, when he had need, and was an hungred, he, and they that were with him? How he went into the house of God in the days of Abiathar the high priest, and did eat the shewbread, which is not lawful to eat but for the priests, and gave also to them which were with him? And he said unto them, The sabbath was made for man, and not man for the sabbath: Therefore the Son of man is Lord also of the sabbath.

MARK 3:4-6

And he saith unto them, Is it lawful to do good on the sabbath days, or to do evil? to save life, or to kill? But they held their peace. And when he had looked round about on them with anger, being grieved for the hardness of their hearts, he saith unto the man, Stretch forth thine hand. And he stretched it out: and his hand was restored whole as the other. And the Pharisees went forth, and straightway took counsel with the Herodians against him, how they might destroy him.

LUKE 6:1–11

And it came to pass on the second sabbath after the first, that he went through the corn, fields; and his disciples plucked the ears of corn, and did eat, rubbing them in their hands. And certain of the Pharisees said unto them, Why do ye that which is not lawful to do on the sabbath days? And Jesus answering them said, Have ye not read so much as this, what David did, when himself was an hungred, and they which were with him; How he went into the house of God, and did take and eat the shewbread, and gave also to them that were with him; which it is not lawful to eat but for the priests alone? And he said unto them, That the Son of man is Lord also of the sabbath. And it came to pass also on another sabbath, that he entered into the synagogue and taught: and there was a man whose right hand was withered. And the scribes and Pharisees watched him, whether he would heal on the sabbath day; that they might find an accusation against him. But he knew their thoughts, and said to the man which had the withered hand, Rise up, and stand forth in the midst. And he arose and stood forth. Then said Jesus unto them, I will ask you one thing; Is it lawful on the sabbath days to do good, or to do evil? to save life, or to destroy it? And looking round about upon them all, he said unto the man, Stretch forth thy hand. And he did so: and his hand was restored whole as the other. And they were filled with madness; and communed one with another what they might do to Jesus.

JOHN 20:19

Then the same day at evening, being the first day of the week, when the doors were shut where the disciples were assembled for fear of the Jews, came Jesus and stood in the midst, and saith unto them, Peace be unto you.

ACTS 1:12

Then returned they unto Jerusalem from the mount called Olivet, which is from Jerusalem a sabbath day's journey.

ACTS 15:24

Forasmuch as we have heard, that certain which went out from us have troubled you with words, subverting your souls, saying, Ye must be circumcised, and keep the law: to whom we gave no such commandment: It seemed good unto us, being assembled with one accord, to send chosen men unto you with our beloved Barnabas and Paul, Men that have hazarded their lives for the name of our Lord Jesus Christ. We have sent therefore Judas and Silas, who shall also tell you the same things by mouth. For it seemed good to the Holy Ghost, and to us, to lay upon you no greater burden than these necessary things; That ye abstain from meats offered to idols, and from blood, and from things strangled, and from fornication: from which if ye keep yourselves, ye shall do well. Fare ye well.

ROMANS 13:8-10

Owe no man any thing, but to love one another: for he that loveth another hath fulfilled the law. For this, Thou shalt not commit adultery, Thou shalt not kill, Thou shalt not steal, Thou shalt not bear false witness, Thou shalt not covet; and if there be any other commandment, it is briefly comprehended in this saying, namely, Thou shalt love thy neighbour as thyself. Love worketh no ill to his neighbour: therefore love is the fulfilling of the law.

1 CORINTHIANS 16:2

Upon the first day of the week let every one of you lay by him in store, as God hath prospered him, that there be no gatherings when I come.

COLOSSIANS 2:16–17

Let no man therefore judge you in meat, or in drink, or in respect of an holyday, or of the new moon, or of the sabbath days: Which are a shadow of things to come; but the body is of Christ.

HEBREWS 4:1–11

Let us therefore fear, lest, a promise being left us of entering into his rest, any of you should seem to come short of it. For unto us was the gospel preached, as well as unto them: but the word preached did not profit them, not being mixed with faith in them that heard it. For we which have believed do enter into rest, as he said, As I have sworn in my wrath, if they shall enter into my rest: although the works were finished from the foundation of the world. For he spake in a certain place of the seventh day on this wise, And God did rest the seventh day from all his works. And in this place again, If they shall enter into my rest. Seeing therefore it remaineth that some must enter therein, and they to whom it was first preached entered not in because of unbelief: Again, he limiteth a certain day, saying in David, To day, after so long a time; as it is said, To day if ye will hear his voice, harden not your hearts. For if Jesus had given them rest, then would he not afterward have spoken of another day. There remaineth therefore a rest to the people of God. For he that is entered into his rest, he also hath ceased from his own works, as God did from his. Let us labour therefore to enter into that rest, lest any man fall after the same example of unbelief.

To whom does the Sabbath apply?

Do Christians need to observe it?

Saturday or Sunday?

In Genesis 2, God rested on the seventh day. It's interesting to note that the phrase "And the evening and the morning were the seventh day." is not in the text, which tells us that the seventh day never had an ending and, as such, has continued to the present day, and that God has also continued in the day of rest – the sabbath – even to the present day. God blesses the seventh day and makes it holy.

In Exodus 16, God first reveals his command to keep the sabbath to Moses on Mount Sinai. (Which is in Arabia, not Egypt – see Galatians 4:25).

So before then there was no knowledge of it? This would mean that Adam, Moses and Abraham did not observe the sabbath, rather they just obeyed God's direct commands by faith. It is also the first mention that no work is to be done and enough food has to be prepared the day before. The people are also commanded to stay inside their houses and do no work.

The ten commandments, as given in Exodus 20 goes on to expound that no work is done by anybody in the household, including servants, cattle or visitors. God shows the people that the six days of creation and the seventh day of rest is a pattern for them to follow, also reinforcing the fact that he made the world – and all that in them is – in six days.

In Exodus 31, God commands the people to keep the sabbath as it is holy unto them, and observe it as a sign of the covenant between he and them. Anyone breaking the sabbath is to be put to death.

Exodus 35 repeats that the seventh day is a holy day of rest to the Lord and that no work is to be done on that day; anyone breaking this command is to be put to death. The passage also commands no fires are to be lighted on the sabbath.

Nehemiah 9 confirms that the sabbath was MADE KNOWN to the Israelites by Moses, which seems to confirm that Adam, Moses and Abraham didn't know about it.

The Old Testament is pretty clear. The sabbath was given to the Israelites, as a sign of the covenant between them and

God, as a day of rest from ALL work, as a remembrance to God and his work of creation. Anyone breaking the sabbath was to be put to death – to be 'cut off' from among the Israelites. To remember the sabbath is one of the ten commandments.

The Jewish week traditionally is from Sunday to Saturday, Saturday being the sabbath (the last day of the week), which lasts from sunset on Friday until sunset on Saturday. Jewish days start at sunset and have the period of darkness first and then the daytime.

In Matthew 12 Jesus and his disciples are in a cornfield, on the sabbath and are hungry, so they pluck and eat the ears of corn. The Pharisees see this and ask Jesus why his disciples are breaking the law. The interesting thing to note here is: Jesus is out of his house on the sabbath. So are the disciples. As are the Pharisees. What are they doing outside? It is clearly a breech of the Mosiac Law in Exodus 16, wherein the Israelites are commanded not to go outside on the sabbath. Matthew 12 ends with Jesus declaring that he is Lord of the sabbath. The parallel passage in Mark 2 tells us that the sabbath was made for us (man), not man for the sabbath. It was made for our benefit.

In John 20, after the resurrection and on the FIRST day of the week, Jesus walks through walls into a locked room. But he had a physical body!

On a side note here, our resurrection bodies – which will be the same as the Lords – appear to have more than three dimensions! Or they are at least able to move through solid objects. Four dimensions are possibly suggested in Ephesians 3:17-18:

"That Christ may dwell in your hearts by faith; that ye, being rooted and grounded in love, May be able to comprehend with all saints what is the breadth, and length, and depth, and height;"

It's interesting to ponder this, as time, the generally accepted fourth dimension, will cease to exist in eternity. There will be no more sun either as God is light and he will give it to us (Revelation 22).

Acts 15 gives only four commandments to Gentile believers: to abstain from fornication, things strangled, eating blood and eating food offered to idols. There is no mention of keeping the sabbath. Romans 13 repeats many of the ten commandments, and once again the sabbath commandment is missing. This makes sense as Jesus himself is Lord of the sabbath, and if we are in Christ, then we are in the sabbath i.e. we are observing it. We find our rest in Jesus.

1 Corinthians 16 mentions the collection/offering to be made on the first day of the week (Sunday) in preparation of Paul's arrival.

The passage from Colossians 2 seems to settle the Saturday/Sunday argument clearly:

"Let no man therefore judge you in meat, or in drink, or in respect of an holyday, or of the new moon, or of the sabbath days: Which are a shadow of things to come; but the body is of Christ."

As a believer, if you want to meet and have fellowship – that is to say meet as a church – on a Saturday, then go ahead. But if you choose Sunday or any other day for that matter, then you are free to do so, so long as as we do not forsake meeting together as Hebrews 10:25 says:

"Not forsaking the assembling of ourselves together, as the manner of some is; but exhorting one another: and so much the more, as ye see the day approaching."

Fully keeping the sabbath today would be very difficult. As we have already discussed, you would not be allowed out of your house (Exodus 16).

Exodus 35 commands that you cannot kindle a fire. In modern terms this would include not only cooking but no driving a car (you are kindling a fire inside the engine), or using electricity, especially if it comes from gas or coal power stations, which burn fuel to generate electricity. Also, Genesis 20 commands that you may not make anyone else work. In using electricity, someone at the generating company or distribution company will be working.

I don't believe Christians are commanded to keep the sabbath in general, although I do believe there may be a spiritual benefit in doing so, in a similar way for those who choose to fast. Indeed, I do not discount that God himself may speak personally to individual believers in this regard.

In short: the Sabbath was for the Jews. Those who are in Christ are in the Sabbath. I believe there will be a time during the millennial reign where both Jews and Christians will observe the Sabbath.

Anglican Communion/Church of England (CoE)

Church services on Sunday, occasionally in the week.

Roman Catholicism/Orthodox

Church services on Sunday

Baptists

Hold a variety of positions. Majority hold church services on Sunday, whereas the Seventh Day Adventists hold to Saturday (The sabbath day).

Methodists

Church services on Sunday

Transgenderism

GENESIS 1:26-28

And God said, Let us make man in our image, after our likeness: and let them have dominion over the fish of the sea, and over the fowl of the air, and over the cattle, and over all the earth, and over every creeping thing that creepeth upon the earth. So God created man in his own image, in the image of God created he him; male and female created he them. And God blessed them, and God said unto them, Be fruitful, and multiply, and replenish the earth, and subdue it: and have dominion over the fish of the sea, and over the fowl of the air, and over every living thing that moveth upon the earth.

GENESIS 2:21-25

And the LORD God caused a deep sleep to fall upon Adam, and he slept: and he took one of his ribs, and closed up the flesh instead thereof; And the rib, which the LORD God had taken from man, made he a woman, and brought her unto the man. And Adam said, This is now bone of my bones, and flesh of my flesh: she shall be called Woman, because she was taken out of Man. Therefore shall a man leave his father and his mother, and shall cleave unto his wife: and they shall be one flesh. And they were both naked, the man and his wife, and were not ashamed.

GENESIS 4:1–2

And Adam knew Eve his wife; and she conceived, and bare Cain, and said, I have gotten a man from the LORD. And she again bare his brother Abel. And Abel was a keeper of sheep, but Cain was a tiller of the ground.

GENESIS 5:1–2

This is the book of the generations of Adam. In the day that God created man, in the likeness of God made he him; Male and female created he them; and blessed them, and called their name Adam, in the day when they were created.

DEUTERONOMY 22:5

The woman shall not wear that which pertaineth unto a man, neither shall a man put on a woman's garment: for all that do so are abomination unto the LORD thy God.

DEUTERONOMY 32:4

He is the Rock, his work is perfect: for all his ways are judgment: a God of truth and without iniquity, just and right is he.

2 SAMUEL 22:31

As for God, his way is perfect; the word of the LORD is tried: he is a buckler to all them that trust in him.

PSALM 18:30-32

As for God, his way is perfect: the word of the LORD is tried: he is a buckler to all those that trust in him. For who is God save the LORD? or who is a rock save our God? It is God that girdeth me with strength, and maketh my way perfect.

PSALM 19:7-9

The law of the LORD is perfect, converting the soul: the testimony of the LORD is sure, making wise the simple. The statutes of the LORD are right, rejoicing the heart: the commandment of the LORD is pure, enlightening the eyes. The fear of the LORD is clean, enduring for ever: the judgments of the LORD are true and righteous altogether.

PSALM 104:30

Thou sendest forth thy spirit, they are created: and thou renewest the face of the earth.

PSALM 119:73

Thy hands have made me and fashioned me: give me understanding, that I may learn thy commandments.

JEREMIAH 17:9-10

The heart is deceitful above all things, and desperately wicked: who can know it? I the LORD search the heart, I try the reins, even to give every man according to his ways, and according to the fruit of his doings.

MATTHEW 19:4-5

And he answered and said unto them, Have ye not read, that he which made them at the beginning made them male and female, And said, For this cause shall a man leave father and mother, and shall cleave to his wife: and they twain shall be one flesh?

MATTHEW 19:12

For there are some eunuchs, which were so born from their mother's womb: and there are some eunuchs, which were made eunuchs of men: and there be eunuchs, which have made themselves eunuchs for the kingdom of heaven's sake. He that is able to receive it, let him receive it.

MATTHEW 6:25–29

Therefore I say unto you, Take no thought for your life, what ye shall eat, or what ye shall drink; nor yet for your body, what ye shall put on. Is not the life more than meat, and the body than raiment? Behold the fowls of the air: for they sow not, neither do they reap, nor gather into barns; yet your heavenly Father feedeth them. Are ye not much better than they? Which of you by taking thought can add one cubit unto his stature? And why take ye thought for raiment? Consider the lilies of the field, how they grow; they toil not, neither do they spin: And yet I say unto you, That even Solomon in all his glory was not arrayed like one of these.

MARK 10:6

But from the beginning of the creation God made them male and female.

LUKE 12:22-24

And he said unto his disciples, Therefore I say unto you, Take no thought for your life, what ye shall eat; neither for the body, what ye shall put on. The life is more than meat, and the body is more than raiment. Consider the ravens: for they neither sow nor reap; which neither have storehouse nor barn; and God feedeth them: how much more are ye better than the fowls?

JOHN 1:1-3

In the beginning was the Word, and the Word was with God, and the Word was God. The same was in the beginning with God. All things were made by him; and without him was not any thing made that was made.

JOHN 14:5-6

Thomas saith unto him, Lord, we know not whither thou goest; and how can we know the way? Jesus saith unto him, I am the way, the truth, and the life: no man cometh unto the Father, but by me.

ROMANS 3:10-11

As it is written, There is none righteous, no, not one: There is none that understandeth, there is none that seeketh after God.

GALATIANS 1:15-16

But when it pleased God, who separated me from my mother's womb, and called me by his grace, To reveal his Son in me, that I might preach him among the heathen; immediately I conferred not with flesh and blood:

GALATIANS 3:28

There is neither Jew nor Greek, there is neither bond nor free, there is neither male nor female: for ye are all one in Christ Jesus.

EPHESIANS 4:11-15

And he gave some, apostles; and some, prophets; and some, evangelists; and some, pastors and teachers; For the perfecting of the saints, for the work of the ministry, for the edifying of the body of Christ: Till we all come in the unity of the faith, and of the knowledge of the Son of God, unto a perfect man, unto the measure of the stature of the fulness of Christ: That we henceforth be no more children, tossed to and fro, and carried about with every wind of doctrine, by the sleight of men, and cunning craftiness, whereby they lie in wait to deceive; But speaking the truth in love, may grow up into him in all things, which is the head, even Christ:

JAMES 1:5-7

If any of you lack wisdom, let him ask of God, that giveth to all men liberally, and upbraideth not; and it shall be given him. But let him ask in faith, nothing wavering. For he that wavereth is like a wave of the sea driven with the wind and tossed. For let not that man think that he shall receive any thing of the Lord. A double minded man is unstable in all his ways.

What does God say about gender?

Does God make mistakes?

What about eunuchs?

How should Christians deal with transgender people?

Until fairly recently the terms gender and sex were used synonymously, with gender referring to the social and cultural differences between the sexes, and sex referring to the genetic and biological differences. Gender can be understood as man or women, sex can be understood as male or female.

Today there are those who seek to differentiate them into two different things, distinct and separate from one another. For the sake of this discussion, I will use sex and gender synonymously.

Today we live in a fallen, corrupted world, as result of Adam and Eve's disobedience. Sin has entered the creation and permeates everything: biologically, physically, mentally and spiritually. But in the beginning God made all things perfect, and with the creation of man on the sixth day, it was (all) very good. The passages from 2 Samuel 22, Psalm 18 and Psalm 19 tell us that God is perfect in ALL things. In other words he DOES NOT make mistakes.

Genesis 1 tells us that God created mankind in his image, male and female. Two opposite but complimentary sexes.

And because there are two, the bible says "...he created them." He then blesses them and commands them to procreate, and "...replenish (fill) the earth, and subdue it". The Bible here is illustrating basic biology in that only a man and a women, coming together in sexual union, can produce offspring.

Genesis 4 confirms this when it states: "And Adam knew (had sex with) Eve his wife; and she conceived, and bare Cain."

So we have a male (man) having sex with a female (woman) and producing children. In essence, biological distinction between the sexes. There is no mention of gender. On a side note, in Genesis 2 we have the creation of Eve from one of Adam's ribs. The rib was taken from his side, rather than from his feet (that he may keep Eve down trodden) or from his head (that Eve may rule his head), so that they could stand side by side, equal in value, dignity and worth.

In Deuteronomy 22, God commands an observable distinction between the sexes:

"The woman shall not wear that which pertaineth unto a man, neither shall a man put on a woman's garment: for all that do so are abomination unto the LORD thy God."

Women should not wear men's clothing. Nor should men wear women's clothing. It makes God sick. What we need to consider here are cultural and societal norms. For example, in warmer climates, men can often be found wearing a tunic or skirt type piece of clothing that in colder climates, like the West, would be considered female clothing. The only real difference being the shaping of the garment: the mens' being shapeless and billowing and the ladies' being much more fitted to the female form. The Scottish kilt as worn by men is quite different to the version worn by women. In modern society now and especially in the West there has been a lot of experimentation and crossing over in fashion. Women wear trousers. Yes, women's trousers but still trousers. There are even certain fashion designers attempting to push men's skirts.

In the of reading Deuteronomy 22, the use of pertaineth certainly has the sense of dressing up or attempting to pass as the opposite gender. My wife often borrows my sweater

251

if I leave one lying about on a chair for example, when she is cold and can't be bothered to get her own. Similarly I may borrow my wife's coat to dash out to the car in the rain. I don't believe this to be in contravention to this law, the motivation behind the action is clearly not to deceive or obscure one's appearance. Drag queens and kings on the other hand, I believe would be in contravention to the law. As would transgendered people who have gone a step further than just wearing the clothes of the opposite sex, in actually claim to be the opposite sex, denying the reality of their birth gender.

There are some who use the passage in Luke 12 to argue the Deuteronomy 22 no longer applies now.

Luke 12:22-24 states: "And he said unto his disciples, Therefore I say unto you, Take no thought for your life, what ye shall eat; neither for the body, what ye shall put on. The life is more than meat, and the body is more than raiment. Consider the ravens: for they neither sow nor reap; which neither have storehouse nor barn; and God feedeth them: how much more are ye better than the fowls?"

This passage is clearly saying do not worry about your life, food or clothing. That God will provide for you. It is not saying that as a disciple one is free to abandon gender-specific clothing norms.

How do we understand eunuchs? Matthew 19 speaks into this. Eunuchs in today's understanding are people who have had surgical procedures rendering them unable to reproduce, – or in the vernacular – having their 'tubes' cut or tied.

Jesus says in Matthew 19 that there are those who are born eunuchs, i.e. people who are born male or female – who for some reason be it chromosomal or physical are unable to have sexual relations and reproduce; that there are people who have been made eunuchs by man i.e. surgically castrated; and those that choose to be eunuchs for the sake of the kingdom i.e. they choose to be celibate.

There are people who are born intersex, with both sets of genitalia or ambiguous genitalia, or with chromosomal errors like XXY, XYY for example. How does these people fit in with the gender binary? Well, as image bearers of God and precious in his sight, they are worthy of respect but something clearly went wrong at conception, or during pregnancy and true intersex people make up less than 1% of transgendered people, the remaining 99% are biologically male or female but claim to be the opposite sex.

In the rare occasion of human hermaphroditism, the individuals are infertile and cannot fertilize themselves but may be able to carry a baby if they have a womb or fertilize another if they have a functioning penis. These genetic anomalies might be attributed to genetic load. We are hundreds of generations down from Adam and Eve and, as previously mentioned, sin has pervaded everything even down to a genetic level. This may in part be the reason Moses forbade the Israelites from marrying close relatives.

Throughout the old and new testaments, words such as womb are always associate with female nouns: woman, mother, wife. For example Galatians 1:15-16 reads:

"But when it pleased God, who separated me from my mother's womb, and called me by his grace, To reveal his

Son in me, that I might preach him among the heathen; immediately I conferred not with flesh and blood."

Clearly it is only (biological) females who can be women, mothers or wives; who have the capacity and anatomy for childbirth. Stating such a fact today is seen as controversial and even worse, transphobic.

Galatians 3:28 reads: "There is neither Jew nor Greek, there is neither bond nor free, there is neither male nor female: for ye are all one in Christ Jesus."

Here we have binary and opposite pairings, Jews and Greeks, bond (slaves) and free, male and female, used to illustrate that we are ALL one in Christ.

The Bible only refers to women having wombs. Furthermore, God is there at the moment of conception. God knows the person before conception. He knows whether the child will be male or female.

So is transgenderism a mental illness? Well, it was once called gender dysphoria. It was accepted as a medical condition but now people want their condition/delusion affirmed as reality i.e. no longer an illness but an identity. Whilst one is free to believe whatever one likes that person doesn't have the right to tell another what to think.

The passage from JAMES 1 seems pertinent here:

"If any of you lack wisdom, let him ask of God, that giveth to all men liberally, and upbraideth not; and it shall be given him. But let him ask in faith, nothing wavering. For he that wavereth is like a wave of the sea driven with the wind and tossed. For let not that man think that he shall receive any thing of the Lord. A double minded man is unstable in all his ways."

The bible is saying here that if you are lacking in wisdom – or are confused about something – pray and ask God. He will not criticize you for asking, and gives liberally. And it goes on to say that a man of two minds (two positions) is unstable in all his ways. Without a firm foundation one could say.

Self identification is dangerous. Leaving it up to an individual to decide their truth would ultimately make truth subjective. As Jeremiah 17 tells us, "The heart is deceitful above all things, and desperately wicked: who can know it?" We need a standard of truth that is outside ourselves or else judgement is flawed because of our sinful nature. Romans 3:10 tells us "As it is written, There is none righteous, no, not one."

We are all sinners affected by sin. Furthermore, John 1 tells us

"ALL things were made through him."

Jesus (God) said in Genesis 1 and Mark 10 in the beginning "God made them male and female." And he should know! Indeed, he is the ultimate authority.

"And he gave some, apostles; and some, prophets; and some, evangelists; and some, pastors and teachers; For the perfecting of the saints, for the work of the ministry, for the edifying of the body of Christ: Till we all come in the unity of the faith, and of the knowledge of the Son of God, unto a perfect man, unto the measure of the stature of the fulness of Christ: That we henceforth be no more children, tossed to and fro, and carried about with every wind of doctrine, by the sleight of men, and cunning craftiness, whereby they lie in wait to deceive; But speaking the truth in love, may grow up into him in all things, which is the head, even Christ:" Ephesians 4:11–15.

In examining our final passage from Ephesians 4, it is clear that Christians should tell the truth on these issues. The truth is much more loving than a lie, even if it is upsetting or offensive at first. No matter what people are struggling with, we are all image bearers of God, and precious in his sight. And we all need a relationship with him that can only be had through the Lord Jesus Christ, by repentance and faith.

In short: human beings cannot trust their own heart (subjective feelings), we need an objective truth outside ourselves, unaffected by sin. We need Jesus! And Jesus clearly said that he made them male and female: binary, opposite and complimentary; Biological sexes. Gender as separated from sex is a modern invention of sinful mankind, a sinful heart without an absolute standard of truth. Any confusion is a result of sin and living in a fallen world. Christians should be bold in presenting Biblical truth in love.

Anglican Communion/Church of England (CoE)
Some churches are now offering transgender baptisms. Church of England has accepted transgender priests since the year 2000.

Roman Catholicism/Orthodox
At present, reject transgenderism.

Baptists
In The Southern Baptist Convention and generally, transgenderism is rejected.

Methodists
Accept transgenderism.

Printed in Great Britain
by Amazon